CONTINUUM ONE HUNDREDS SERIES

100 IDEAS
FOR SUPPLY
TEACHERS

PRIMARY SCHOOL EDITION

Michael Parry

continuum

I am most grateful to Christina Garbutt for her cheerful, positive encouragment, her patience and guidance and for all her valuable advice in helping me with my writing, and to Mary for her support and enthusiasm as I worked.

Continuum International Publishing Group

The Tower Building	80 Maiden Lane
11 York Road	Suite 704
London	New York
SE1 7NX	NY10038

www.continuumbooks.com

British Library Cataloguing-in-Publication Data
A catalogue record for this book is available from the British Library.

ISBN: 0-8264-8988-5 (paperback)

Library of Congress Cataloging-in-Publication Data
A catalog record for this book is available from the Library of Congress.

Typeset by Ben Cracknell Studios
Printed and bound in Great Britain by Ashford Colour Press Ltd, Gosport, Hampshire

CONTENTS

SECTION 4 **Literacy**

SECTION 5 **Numeracy**

SECTION 6 **Science**

SECTION 15 **Behaviour management**

SECTION 16 **Making the most of your day**

As a class teacher I found it beneficial to set the tone for the whole year or the term, or the day or even the session, right from the outset by creating a climate of expectation. I set out for the children the kind of behaviour and work ethic I expected in order to enhance meaningful learning and, in return, what they could expect from me in terms of interesting work, activities, rewards and sanctions. I have developed these techniques over my career and these were enhanced and simplified as my reputation in the school grew. I found that the more I perfected my skills and techniques in creating an interesting and lively learning environment, the easier I found teaching and learning through meaningful interaction with the children who already knew me.

As a supply teacher, however, I found the whole climate very different. I had to remember that I now had to create my own reputation on a daily basis and I also found that it is still perfectly possible to exercise my management skills to the full, as I sampled life working daily in different schools, with a wide range of age groups and abilities. I learned very early on in my career that children must be kept busy, challenged, interested and motivated and they will be happy. It is only when they experience periods of inactivity or the lack of challenge that disruptive behaviour will start.

An essential strategy for you is to 'claim' the classroom for yourself. The children will expect you to be their 'leader' and if you fail to take the lead, the most dominant child will perceive the power vacuum and will move to take over the leadership role and control the environment, pushing behaviour boundaries, causing disruption and disturbing the learning process. If this happens you will have lost the class. It is much easier to avoid this scenario developing than it is to remedy the situation.

Structuring your day

EARLY WORK – ENGAGING ATTENTION, SETTING CHALLENGES

It is very important that the children should begin the day busy. As they enter the classroom they should know that they will be expected to work, therefore as they come in make sure you have starters ready for them. This work should be in the form which engages their attention, challenging them to complete the exercise. An example of such work could be a set of computation exercises graded from simple to complex problems; they could be set words out of which they must make complex sentences which could be related to a specific context for example, holidays, the school play, wildlife preservation or environmental pollution. The effect of this strategy is that you are free to undertake the essentials of daily routines such as registration, collecting letters and money, talking to parents, listening to complaints and worries, giving out instructions or discussing essentials with the classroom assistants and generally taking your place in the classroom. Starters are also a good disciplinary tool because it settles the children, setting the work climate for the rest of the day.

Hint: Make sure the work you set looks attractive, that it is short enough to be completed in the time available and then aim to have enough time for the class to mark the work together.

You have to be flexible to work in the primary sector, and to this end you should be prepared to change, to adapt or to abandon your session mid-stream. If you find that what you have prepared is not working, stop the activity. Tell the children that you are not satisfied, that the session is not working for them and then switch focus. I was taking a Numeracy session as a supply teacher in a school I had not known before and I was expected to teach matrix multiplication, a method with which I was unfamiliar and I discovered, after beginning the session that the class teacher had not prepared the children with any of the basic concepts regarding this method of multiplication. I soon found I was talking to a traumatized, glazed entity; to a child they were all equally shell-shocked. I found I was getting nowhere fast and the children were showing signs of restlessness. I gave up any attempt at following the set work and taught simple multiplication using a two-digit multiplier. Life then got so much easier for all of us. The children were on familiar ground and they went about their work, focused and on task.

Begin the main body of the session with a clear explanation of the concepts you will be leading the children into exploring and learning. Make sure you explain the tasks simply and explicitly and that you check at each stage that the class are following you and that they understand what it is you are saying.

Once you have completed your explanation, ask if the children have understood. Be patient and be prepared to go over the work again just to make sure. Watch the children; the cues you have will be the vacant look, inattention, a lack of focus, fidgeting and the beginnings of unrelated activity. Focus on the individual(s) who asked for the clarification and make sure that when you have gone over the work again you ask them to repeat what you had just explained. Try to spend no more than 15 minutes explaining an idea, then set the children reinforcement work before advancing to the next logical stage.

Always try to include a plenary session which should be used to reinforce the work of each session. This is where you go over the concepts, the ideas, the activities and the learning which took place in the session. Ask the children questions about the session and pick one or two individuals to tell the class what it is they had learned, and use them to crystallize the ideas for those who may still be unsure. It is during this session that you could be leading the class in marking their work.

THE PLENARY SESSION

Learn from every school and every class teacher. Observe techniques and strategies. Watch very carefully to see how the teachers deal with issues such as:

¶ indiscipline in the playground
¶ how the children line up to enter the school
¶ what the teachers do, or the routines they have set, in the classroom for registration, for lining up for play, for assembly or lunchtimes or for simple classroom routines such as preparation for art or other practical subjects
¶ how the children are prepared for changing for PE or Games
¶ how the children are set in workgroups
¶ how the children work in their workgroups – set materials or books for example
¶ the classroom layout – to make sure that all children are able to watch the board
¶ where there may be a table set out especially for the problem child to be isolated in 'time-out'.

This is not intended as an exhaustive or a prescriptive list but as a guide to the sorts of resources/support you might find you can adopt and adapt to make your job and your day less stressful, more productive for you and for the children and, perhaps, your preparedness will enhance your performance and your professional reputation.

Very simply you should:

1 Be prepared – be *over* prepared
2 Be on time
3 Be well dressed – even if the permanent staff look as if they are dressed in an effort to earn 'cred' from their streetwise pupils. I do know from my own experience that kids instinctively perceive a well-turned out adult as a figure of authority to respect. I have personally observed children teasing a supply teacher whose contemporary dress was judged by the streetwise children to be 'too young for such an old person'.
4 Be firm but fair – you should be prepared to execute a threat, promise once made.
5 Always be prepared to admit you are wrong – if you are wrong and the children have seen this.
6 Set out your expectations, either overtly or covertly through rewards and sanctions
7 Demand high standards of work and behaviour
8 Be in control of your class
9 Take a full part in the school as a professional – don't look the other way if you see something amiss
10 Be flexible
11 Have a good, focused working climate with all of the children on task and focused

Above all use your own discretion, but remember that your professional reputation will depend on your performance and this will certainly be a factor determining how full your working diary could be.

Collecting information on the school/class organization

TIMETABLES

¶ Ensure you get a copy of the school timetable which sets out start times, assembly times, break times, lunch times and time for the end of the session.

¶ Make sure you are on time by preparing a little earlier for the scheduled times. You could for example, spend a small part of your break or lunch time finding out where the textbooks are stored or where to find the maths or science equipment. In this way you will know beforehand whether you will need to make adjustments to carry out your plans successfully.

¶ Make sure you know what to do for each of your sessions and where you have to be, how you will get there and what sort of support assistance you can expect for any out-of-class activities. Check out all of this information by talking to the school secretary – if this is your first point of contact, or else ask whoever will show you to your classroom, or else the next best contact will be the classroom assistant – if there is one. You may also be able to work from any notes left for you by the class teacher.

Check on the class routines – does the class have:

- an assembly
- duties of any sort
- practical lessons such as craft, art or design technology
- swimming lessons
- games or PE?

Ask what is expected of you in each case, for example:

- Find out where the assembly is to take place – at what time it is to take place, what is expected of you?
- Ask what your 'duty' entails – where you will be expected to be, what you will be expected to do and the times involved?
- Ask if the practical session is to take place in a room specific to the activity and what materials, equipment, resources and support you can expect.
- In the event that you are expected to leave the school premises – say to support a swimming lesson – ask everything you need to know about transport, support, teaching assistance, timing and expectations.

SPECIAL NEEDS

You will need to know about the Special Educational Needs (SEN) children in the class. Make sure you know what their specific needs are and how these needs are to be met. Some examples of the sorts of needs you might find will be those children:

¶ with learning difficulties
¶ who might not be able to speak English
¶ who might suffer from hearing loss.

In any event you should plan to have work prepared which might be relatively simple tasks such as completing sentences using given words in a list, or simple basic operations in maths.

It might be wise to check especially on allergies of which you will have to be particularly aware, so that you do not inadvertently make physical contact with a child suffering from any nut allergy.

You will generally find this information published in a special folder either in the classroom or in the staffroom; if not ask the member of staff who will direct you to your room and who may know about the SEN register or individuals.

Find out if you will have any classroom assistants working in the room with you. Such assistance will be invaluable; classroom assistants can be particularly helpful and knowledgeable with the special needs of all the children. Make full use of this valuable resource by asking about

¶ individuals and any potential behavioural problems
¶ routines
¶ resources
¶ expected standards of behaviour and work ethic
¶ potential problems and how these are dealt with on a routine basis
¶ any children that are to be withdrawn from the class for learning support and when and how this will take place.

CLASSROOM ASSISTANTS

WORK PLANS

Make sure you have an outline plan of the work you will be expected to cover and be prepared with lots of supplementary work of your own, either to support what you have been left, or in the event that you may not have anything left for you. Class teachers often overlook the fact that the individuals in the class interact very differently with the supply teacher and it is not uncommon therefore that the work left is insufficient to challenge every individual. Look out especially for those children who will rush to complete the work just so that they are free to 'interact' with the rest of the class or with their friends. Always remember that the key to good discipline is in keeping the child interested, focused, on task and actively engaged.

Ask about the policies the school has in place concerning the application of sanctions and back-up to support discipline. You will need to know what to do in the event that you discover a challenging, disruptive individual. Always be prepared to send for a senior member of staff in the event of any difficult and potentially disruptive situation. Remember that you cannot know the circumstances of each and every individual and the causes of their behaviour and it is always wise to ask for support. Generally speaking, your involving the senior staff at the school gives signal of your intent to deal with issues immediately and will support your classroom discipline and establish your expectations for a quiet, purposeful, focused learning climate.

SCHOOL POLICIES

FIRE REGULATIONS

Look out for the fire regulations and details of fire escape and assembly points. While this may not seem entirely pertinent to you, it is an important part of the school policy to test their routines and procedures to include visitors who may not be familiar with the school and therefore most at risk.

It is of critical importance that you are completely responsible for the children in your care and you should therefore be completely prepared so that in the event of a real fire you are able to ensure the safety of your class. To this end you should be aware of how it is you will get your class out to safety in the event of a fire by familiarizing yourself with exits and escape routes, the school fire escape procedures and how any children with special needs may be assisted.

What you need to know

TEACHING THE AGE RANGES

It is good policy that you prepare work to cover the whole of the primary/middle range, especially if you are prepared to teach in primary, junior and middle schools. Obviously, the younger the children you cover, the less academically demanding you make the work and the fewer subjects you will have to prepare for cover.

The age range covered by most primary schools is from 5 to 11, that is Key Stages (KS) 1 and 2. Other variations are the Infant Schools with children ranging in age from 5 to 7 (KS1), separate from the junior schools, taking children in from 7 up to 11(KS2). These split-sites schools do exist but are infrequent because of the costs involved with the management structures. Then there are the first schools, which cater for children ranging in age from 5 to 8 or from 5 to 9. The children then go on to the middle schools, which cater either for the 8 to 12 or the 9 to 13-year-old children.

It may be an easier task if you know the system being operated by the Local Education Authority, in which case you could just prepare for the 6 year groups of the conventional primary school. You will need no more than a small range of worksheets for the core subjects for each level because the class teacher will generally have an ongoing programme for such subjects as history or geography, craft and design technology or science, and you will not be expected to teach complete facets within the 'topic' areas of these subjects.

Once in school, check the resources in the classroom. What you are looking out for will be the essentials such as sets of:

¶ textbooks – for work appropriate to the class
¶ class atlases
¶ dictionaries
¶ copies of the thesaurus

The other resources you could look out for and *which depend on what it is planned* that you will cover will be:

¶ maths resources such as multilink, centicubes, compasses and protractors
¶ scissors
¶ glue sticks
¶ Sellotape
¶ drawing pencils
¶ paints and paintbrushes
¶ water pots
¶ newspaper
¶ sugar paper and card
¶ magnets
¶ bulbs, batteries and leads
¶ visual aids on plants and the human body.

This is not another essential checklist and it is not intended that you should look out for all of these items in every classroom/school in which you will work. My intention is to have you prepared for the eventuality so that you will ask for these resources automatically since they will support some of the work I have suggested elsewhere.

The most informative, valuable, useful and up-to-date sources of information on the curriculum, content and innovation is the DfES at www.standards.dfes.gov.uk and the BBC at www.bbc.co.uk/schools where you will also find lesson plans, ideas, content, resource lists, follow-up, assessment and child-centred interactive content, all easily accessible on their websites. Another good source of ideas on age appropriate content will be found in the range of Study Guides, such as Letts Revision Notes and

Practice Papers, WH Smiths Primary Skills, or the Coordination Group KS2 Study

Take in as much stand-alone work as you can prepare that will require just the simplest of resources which can be adapted for the different ages and abilities. Remember that, in the primary school, you must be prepared to cover the complete range of subjects and you would be well advised to build up a wide range of resources which you can use to teach the age and ability range.

The laissez-faire attitude of letting the supply teacher 'get-on-with-it because they are being paid for it' is very much a thing of the past, and managing the children with dot-to-dot or colouring-in sheets, crosswords, word searches and drawing exercises is now no longer acceptable.

Examine the resources, worksheets and texts which you may find in the classroom. Adapt and absorb any good ideas which you know will help you to consolidate and to hone your skills. Get copies of any worksheets you know will help you because you want to capitalize on good ideas and not have to invent these ideas yourself. Your aim is to travel light but to deliver like a heavy-weight, providing the children with interesting, challenging, worthwhile work which keeps them focused and on task.

Good resources for motivating pupils are:

- stars, a stamp or stickers with which to reward good work
- a whistle for your PE and games sessions
- a little bell to place on the desk which you use to condition the children to respond to when you wish their focused attention. The strategy is to take the bell out of your bag as you introduce yourself, and tell the children that when they hear the sound of the bell they are to stop whatever they are doing and listen to you because you want to talk to them about what they are doing. I found this to be a good strategy wherever I went.

RESOURCES FOR MOTIVATING THE PUPILS

You may well be left a full set of lessons to work to and find that there is more than enough to keep the children challenged and on task. In any event it is always wise to have more than sufficient back-up material of your own as this may not be the case in the event of an unplanned absence.

Remember that you will be expected to be independent and self-sufficient and not require too much input by the permanent staff, all of whom will be concerned with getting their own preparation in place. Everyone will expect to help you with the basic organization of school routines but no one will be prepared to help make up your lesson plans for you.

You will find that most primary and middle schools timetable the following subjects, some of which you will be expected to cover:

1 literacy
2 numeracy
3 science
4 history
5 geography
6 RE
7 art
8 craft/design technology
9 music
10 dance
11 PE
12 games

Put together a small bank of resource material relevant to the primary age range and which you should be able to draw upon as needed. The sorts of material you should include in your resource bank could include some of the following:

¶ a file of your own graded worksheets in maths and literacy
¶ a resource bank of commercial material in maths and English
¶ a copy of a spelling list – perhaps Schonell's Essential Spelling List

- a videotape of a history, geography or science content recorded from broadcast material or using material from Letts, Smiths, or the Coordination Group Publications of study guides and material
- a CD or audiotape of instrumental music for music and dance.

Literacy

LITERACY WARM UP

For the warm-up exercise, prepare a list of 5 words. Instruct the children look up these words in a dictionary then tell them that they should write sentences of their own using these words. For the younger or less able children, include cloze exercises in the form of worksheets with, for example, complete sentences from which key words have been omitted. Set the children the exercise of choosing a word from a list you have included on the page which will make the sentence make sense. As an extension exercise, you could have the children use their dictionaries to find the meanings of the words they have used.

Examples you might use for the warm-up exercise for the more able/Level 4 pupils could be:

¶ furnish
¶ perfect
¶ beneath
¶ hasten
¶ inspect

Give the children an opening sentence which will require them to use one word from your list, e.g.:

'I will be coming around the class to _____ your work after five minutes.'

Make it clear that they can only use a word from your list.

A list of words you could set for the least able might include:

¶ creep
¶ shine
¶ grand
¶ mole
¶ lace

Hint: Get yourself a copy of the latest Schonell's Spelling List and choose words appropriate to the age range you teach. Select those words which are not likely to be commonly used by the children so that it will be necessary for them to use the dictionary.

Once you have begun with the warm-up exercise, you should aim to have the children get down to some serious writing.

Have the children explore root words. Tell the children that a 'root word' is a word to which we can add beginnings which we call prefixes or endings, the suffixes. Give them examples:

Cent centipede, centimetre, centicubes, century, centurion, centigrade

Get the children to use the dictionary to find out how many words they can form from the following root words:

1 extra
2 free
3 bob

An extension exercise you could set for the most able would be for them to make up sentences from the words they find.

Make sure that the children actually know how to use a dictionary and lead them through a word search of one of your set words. Schonell's does break down words suitable to the different age ranges and you could use this breakdown to illustrate the use of the dictionary.

You will not be expected to carry around a class set of dictionaries or any other class books, and hopefully the school will have sufficient copies available in the class. If this is not the case then ask for a class set to be made available to you.

Begin by introducing yourself to the children – give them a thumbnail sketch of yourself; remember to keep it short and simple. Outline the sort of things you are interested in such as

¶ your likes or dislikes about school
¶ why you like teaching
¶ the type of music you enjoy or your hobbies
¶ Be careful not to allow a debate: your objective is to give them an example of what you expect from them in writing
¶ Tell them that you would like to read about who might like or dislike school, who might find what subject interesting and why, or who might be a member of a large or small family, what range of hobbies there are in the class and so on.

Discuss what 'interesting' might mean so that the children will all be working from a common under-standing. Get the children to suggest what it is that they would find interesting about people and write these ideas on the board, OHT or Interactive White Board (IWB) and add to the words and ideas as you warm up the class.

The rationale for using yourself as a subject to elicit ideas is to give the children a glimpse of your personality – the 'you' behind the face of 'yet another supply teacher'. You are also giving the children a good, clear outline of how to write their essay and ideas to include.

Hint: Stay away from the controversial subjects such as football teams and pop groups, because raising these issues will simply give the children the perfect excuse to initiate a debate which will be bound to generate a lot of excitement, rivalry, much discussion and most certainly it will provide the opportunity for some children in the class to exploit the situation by talking too much and ensuring little time is left for writing.

Discuss briefly what you see as the place for school in the life of any individual – yourself? A child?

Begin by discussing the purpose of school. Ask the children to think about, then write what they believe are their expectations of school. Stimulate thought by writing some key words on the board and have the children brainstorm ideas associated with each word. Use for example:

- Learning – why do we learn, what do we learn, how is learning best achieved, what do they think is easy to learn and what difficult, where does most learning take place, is there a *real* learning – is learning about subjects or about how to behave?
- Fun – should school be fun, how can fun and learning be put together, is there a different kind of fun in school compared to home or outside school, should fun be kept for outside school?
- Friends – is the school a place where you can expect to make friends, how do you make friends in school, what is a good friend, do many children have friends from outside school, are these friends different – how?
- Is the school somewhere to go while their parents are at work – how many people see this as a reason for school, what do parents think a school should do, what do children think a school should do, is the school purely to look after children, what is the real job of the teachers?
- Is the school somewhere to go because it is required by law – is this a sort of punishment, or is it a special privilege because so many children in the world have to pay for their own education and so many more children in many countries have no schools and no teachers from whom they can learn?

Sum up some of the responses from this discussion. Ask the children to write about what they think from the ideas coming out of these points and get them to articulate, in written mode, what they actually think about school and to rationalize their place in and purpose of being in school.

WRITING ABOUT SUBJECTS

Have the children write about their preferences for school subjects.

The objective for this particular piece of written work is to get the children to discuss their best/worst subject/ activity in school – why they like/dislike it, and ask for any suggestions about what they might like as a subject to learn about in school. You should intend that this discussion stage is used to help the children to:

¶ assimilate and understand the idea
¶ begin to formulate their own ideas
¶ articulate their own ideas.

Remember to keep this stage short and well managed so that you keep the discussion focused. Make sure that the children clearly understand what it is you want from them and get them to write freely about what they think and feel.

Show them how you would like them to set out their writing:

¶ choose your favourite subject – or your worst subject
¶ explain what it is you find 'good' or 'bad' about this subject
¶ what is it that makes the subject enjoyable or not so enjoyable?
¶ what changes would you make if you could make any changes?

Hint: It has been my experience that children have very strong feeling about school and certain subjects, sometimes based on negative experiences such as poor teaching, personality clashes, parental influences or sibling perceptions. In the main, their dislike of a subject area usually stems from their lack of competence or confidence generally arising out of misinformation, misunderstanding and misconception. Very often a child will say they 'don't like it' but cannot rationalize this dislike. It is useful to know these likes and dislikes because you may well be able to rationalize this dislike to unlock or break this self-perpetuating chain of irrational dislike by showing the child how easy or pleasurable the subject can be made.

Begin this discussion stage by asking the children about rules using the following as a guide:

¶ what are rules?
¶ where would they expect to find rules?
¶ why are there rules?
¶ does the school have rules?
¶ do they have class rules?
¶ are there rules outside school?

Get the children to write about what they think of rules and how what they have discussed has helped them to think more clearly about rules and how this affects everyone.

Stretch the more able by asking them what changes they might like to make in an ideal situation.

Hint: Asking about rules is always a good strategy to have the children work collectively to remember the work the school has already undertaken to establish good behaviour, and you can use this exercise to remind the children of how they should behave.

Bear in mind that the most important factor facilitating learning is the safe, ordered, purposeful classroom. You can then remind the children that your role is to teach, not to supervise, baby-mind or entertain and what you want is the kind of behaviour and work commitment which their class teacher will expect.

WRITING ABOUT RULES

IDEA 24

A FAIRY STORY

It is good to begin this exercise with a discussion. Ask the children for example, to think about whether there are such things as Hobbits, or Borrowers or Fairies . . . Why . . . ? Why not . . . ?

Have ready, a passage or two copied from Tolkien, Rowling, Pratchett or Bradman that describe these mythical beings which you can then read to the class to give them an example. It might be useful to have a copy of a book from one of these authors to show the children.

At the end of the discussion stage, get the children to write their own thoughts about how and where these writers get their ideas. As an extension exercise you should get the children to write a very short story of their own, using their imagination to create a myth or fairytale.

Hint: The idea here is to have the children think about how imagination can work and how it is that some imaginative ideas can captivate, entertain and enthuse and that they can also generate ideas, thought and may even give rise to a way of life as, for example the 'Trekkies' who follow *Star Trek*.

Take a story book in to read to the class as a stimulus or example: *The Hobbit*, *The Borrowers*, *The BFG*, *Peter Pan*, *The Lion, the Witch and the Wardrobe*, any of the Harry Potter books, *His Dark Materials*, *Stig of the Dump*, *Charlotte's Web* or work of similar genre from any of the authors I have already outlined above.

Read a short extract, then:

1   ask the children about
    a   the main characters
    b   the plot or story line
    c   the setting – where it is taking place – time . . .
2   give the children about 5 minutes to talk about how they think the
    a   main characters behave
    b   the setting makes the story interesting
    c   pace of the story
    d   story should end.
3   ask the children to write a suitable ending to the story/the chapter. Ask them to include an interesting twist which can lead to a new adventure. This way they may well be encouraged to use their imagination more than simply to find an 'ending' – since endings are so final!

A BEDTIME STORY

Set the less able to writing a short story which you would like to use as a bedtime story for your niece/son/daughter. Give the children a printed guide along the lines I have set out below, with the set headings under which there is a space for them to write a guided piece, putting each of the three stages into outlined boxes:

THE SETTING – INTRODUCTION

¶ In an old cottage at the end of the lane there lived a very old lady and her . . .

THE PLOT/STORY – MAIN BODY

¶ It was early on a Wednesday morning that she heard the knock on her door and . . .

THE RESOLUTION – CONCLUSION

¶ It had been a very long time since the old lady had had such a wonderful surprise and she . . .

Instruct the children that they are to think up a story with the parts which will fit into the three boxes and to write at least two sentences for each of the boxes.

The objective of this session is to tie up/round off and reinforce the concepts you have aimed to develop during the lesson. You should plan to use the work of one of the children whom you might have supervised, or overheard or whose work you might already have marked or read. Discuss the ideas raised, say why you chose this work and invite comment and discussion.

Plan this stage of the lesson by getting the children to:

¶ finish their writing
¶ prepare the children to discuss their own ideas
¶ ask for any child who would like to share their ideas – on issues from the writing session
¶ ask for any differing views or for agreement
¶ conclude the session by highlighting the consensus or differences
¶ give praise for those whose contributions have given pause for thought
¶ leave the children with the idea that they can go beyond the confines of your lesson – that they can continue the idea even if you are not present
¶ aim to complete this component of the lesson in 15 to 20 minutes.

I would advise you to focus on having the children produce a piece of good quality written work of a standard appropriate to the age range. Written work will not only illustrate what it is you have been working on with the class but the children will also feel that they have achieved something and that they have something to show of their time with you. You may also find that a written piece of work of quality might also lead to further exploration by the class teacher and class at a later time. Focus this facet of the lesson on getting the children to articulate their thoughts, the problems they may have encountered in applying the aspects of *language* in the literacy session. Have the children share their learning or the various strategies they may have used in undertaking the set exercise.

Numeracy

NUMERACY WARM UP

For this exercise you should write up a series of simple equations focusing on the nature of number in which one of the essential components is missed out, for example:

$$5 \times \underline{\quad} = 35$$
$$\underline{\quad} + 8 = 14$$
$$\underline{\quad} + 36 = 90$$
$$\underline{\quad} - 60 = 140$$
$$8 \times \underline{\quad} = 72$$

You should set about 10 of these equations giving the children a time limit of 5 minutes for completion, telling them that at the end of the time you will be going over the answers. It is really important to go over the work at the end of the set time, giving the answers and asking the children for their workings out, which you should share with the class. This exercise is truly useful in that you are able to see how the children *think* and solve the problem. Another major use for this is that the less able or the slower thinker may be encouraged to see that she/he is thinking along the right lines, or they may well also find that they could make use of the workings offered by the class.

Hint: It is very important that you set a time limit for completion so that the children know that they have a challenge to work to complete the set exercise. Keep strictly to the time limit whether the children have all finished or not, and *teach* the solutions. Focus on reinforcing the concept of reverse operations so that, taking **8 × ? = 72** for example, show that 72 **divided** by 8 will also give you the answer because you are finding out how many groups of **8** there are in **72**.

The first thing you should expect in the primary classroom is that there will be a wide spread of ability and understanding, especially in numeracy. There are schools which set the classes for numeracy but even in these set groups you will find a wide range of ability. You will find that if you begin with what the children are most familiar they will feel more confident and will be more focused and more motivated because they feel they will be able to complete the work. Beginning with a lesson on ways to add, subtract, multiply and divide numbers will have the children on familiar ground and you will be able to:

THE BASIC OPERATIONS

¶ reinforce learning
¶ correct misconceptions
¶ provide a focus for effort
¶ motivate the children to complete the set tasks.

Begin your session with an explanation that the four basic operations are simple ways of making numbers bigger or smaller. Show them different methods by which they can add or subtract and then get them work on their own to complete the set exercises.

For addition you could try these two methods:

$$260 + 54 + 4112$$

line up the units' digits

$$
\begin{array}{r}
260 \\
54 \\
+ \ 4112 \\
\hline
4426 \\
{\scriptstyle 1}
\end{array}
$$

Another method you could try would be to work from the left – adding the most significant figures first:

$$
\begin{array}{r}
374 \\
+ \ 27 \\
\hline
300 \\
90 \\
11 \\
\hline
401
\end{array}
$$

For subtraction try – 'exchanging'

$$583$$
$$- 147$$

Take one ten from the 80 tens and exchange to make 13 units
now subtract 7 units from the 13 units

or try this:

$205 - 97$

From 97 up to 200 $= 103$
From 205 to 200 $= 5$
So the answer is $ 108$

Look also at the examples I have set out for you in Idea 34 on Decimal computation.

Once you have given them an introduction, do just another three worked examples on the board/screen then have the children work on computation exercises from worksheets or from their textbooks. You might find it useful to have your own worksheets and you could build these up using the examples I have set out below which are focused on the basic operation of addition.

Give the younger or the less able children simple computation involving units and tens, although you should remember that the older and more able children should be challenged using hundreds and thousands as appropriate. Don't expect they will know or even 'remember' how to undertake these basic operations; go over the workings in as interesting a way as you can – try the two methods I have suggested above. Set the children a series of 10 progressively more challenging computations. You could, for example, use three-digit numbers or three discrete numbers as in:

$$198 + 209 =$$
$$427 + 28 + 954 =$$

Make up a few working examples along these lines.

Hints: Show the children how to set out the figures in place value columns and then how to add the figures within these columns. Explain the distinctions between each of the value headings.

In the case of the basic operation of subtraction, show this as the inverse of addition. Show them how to set out subtraction problems and how to remove one quantity from another by decomposition, or as I set out above – *exchanging*. You could ask how they have been taught – find out what methods they have been shown and what they usually do, then use these methods to reinforce their learning. Get the children to explain because the children feel more secure using the methods they know and this will reinforce their understanding of the processes of multiplication and division. A good strategy to structuring the children's activity is *always* give them between two and three worked examples before expecting them to work independently.

FRACTIONS USING SHAPES

Present the children with the concept of fractions in practical terms. Explain that a fraction is a part of a discrete whole. Find fractions of shapes for example or use fractions of quantities. Introduce these as common fractions. Make this a visual practical session. Show how the whole may be divided into an equal number of parts – the denominator. Ask them to shade in one part, three parts or parts appropriate to the number of parts into which the whole has been divided. Once they have done this, ask them now to say how many parts have not been shaded in so that they can see the relationship between the parts shaded, those unshaded and the whole itself.

FRACTIONS OF SHAPE, EXAMPLE 1:

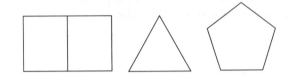

Divide these shapes into two equal parts, the first one has been done for you, then shade in one part out of two – write it like this: 1/2

FRACTIONS OF SHAPE, EXAMPLE 2:

Shade in 2/3 – that is 2 parts out of the 3

Shade in 3/5 – that is 3 parts out of the 5

Shade in 3/4 – that is 3 parts out of the 4

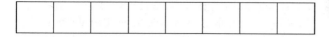

Shade in 7/8 – that is 7 parts out of the 8

Shade in 4/7 – that is 4 parts out of the 7

To do: 1 Now write down *as fractions*, how many parts of the whole are *not* shaded.

2 Draw some of your own shapes shaded to show these fractions:

5/6, 2/5, 6/10, 1/6, 2/3

Hint: Have ready made-up worksheets of drawn rectangles. Have the children do all of the shading and dividing of the shapes on these worksheets as their activity. If you have them to hand, use centicubes or other concrete visual aids such as multifix cubes. Build up a 'stick' of 12 units then use this concrete visual aid to find 1/2 or 1/3 or 1/4.

Have the more able children do their own measuring and drawing of the basic units, copying the 'stick' idea to calculate problems you write out on the board, OHT, IWB or on your photocopy worksheets.

Note: The centicubes are centimetre cubes which lock together and may be used to make visual a wide range of concepts which include fractions, area and volume for example. The multifix are a larger version of the centi-cubes and can be used in much the same way. If you have not met these visual aids before, ask a member of staff for a supply of these cubes. You will find them a real asset.

You should expect the children in Years 5 and 6 (that is the 9 to 11 year olds) to be able to work in abstract without the need for visual aids so they should not need anything more than the set worksheets. Always assume that the children have to be taken back to basics, so use concrete apparatus in your explanation of the processes. Make up a few centicube/multifix 'sticks' of, for example, 12 units. Use these 'sticks' to illustrate adding parts of one 'stick' to parts of another.

Example 1: 1/2 (6 units) of one 'stick' to be added to 4/12 (1/3) of another 'stick'.

Now show the children how to add using fractions of these 'sticks'

1/12 + 3/12, 4/12 + 3/12, 6/12 + 2/12, 5/12 + 7/12, 8/12 + 1/12

Now try them out with subtraction taking a fraction away from part of one 'stick':

6/12 – 2/12, 3/12 – 1/12, 9/12 – 5/12, 7/12 – 5/12, 11/12 – 8/12

Make up your own examples using these ideas but make the work increasingly more challenging as you assess the ability of the class. Always make sure you have work within the topic for a range of abilities. As you work on marking and helping the children, observe and gauge the ability range within the class by examining their books. Look at the standards of completed work and the range of ability within the content recorded in the books.

Hint: Keep to addition and subtraction of common fractions with the inclusion of some mixed fractions. You cannot teach too much because you will not be able to assess absorption and learning, reinforce learning or give follow-up work. It is really important that you make sure that the children know and understand exactly what they are doing before you expect them to begin, since this will ensure that you give them the chance to ask 'how to' and/or 'what am I supposed . . .'. You will also be helping that one child who really has no idea but is afraid to ask!

Learning about equivalent fractions is an essential part of learning and understanding the principle of computation of fractions of different denominations. What the children must learn is that **25 out of 50** is the same as **1 out of 2** or **3 out of 6** or even that **13 out of 39** is the same as **4 out of 12** or **3 out of 9**. This basic concept has huge ramifications for the development of an understanding of addition and subtraction of fractions:

3/4 + 4/7 or 8/9 − 3/5 for example.

For this lesson you should focus on how to convert fractions to give equivalent fractions. Use printed worksheets as in this example, which the children could shade in and keep:

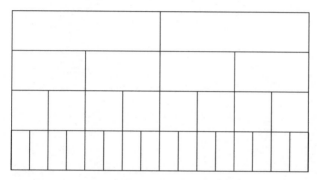

Use the table, as the children shade in the fractions, to explain how equivalent fractions are the same and how fractions may be converted to achieve equivalence.

$$1/2 \ (\times 2/2) = 2/4$$
$$1/2 \ (\times 3/3) = 3/6$$
$$1/2 \ (\times 4/4) = 4/8$$
$$1/2 \ (\times 5/5) = 5/10$$

An example of the sort of exercise you should set is:

$$1/4 = \_/8 = \_/12 = \_/16$$
$$2/3 = \_/6 = \_/9 = 8/\_$$
$$3/5 = \_/10 = \_/15 = 12/\_$$
$$3/4 = \_/8 = 9/\_ = \_/16$$

EQUIVALENT FRACTIONS

Hint: Keep the exercises short enough to engage attention and to prevent the less able children and those who have not yet grasped the concepts having too long to increase their feelings of hopelessness. Always go over the work. Explain and *teach* the processes as you go over the answers. *This strategy also has the added benefit that you will be able to have the children mark their work for you.*

Begin by showing how a decimal fraction is a part of a whole and how these fractions are related to and have equivalence to common fractions but that in decimal fractions the whole is divided into multiples of 10:

> 0.6 = 6 *tenths* = 6/10 (the whole is divided into 10 parts)
> and 0.06 = 6 *hundredths* = 6/100 (the whole is divided into 100 parts)

As you set the children to work explain exactly what it is you expect and how they are to achieve the expectations.

Example 1: Write these fractions as decimal fractions:

> 2/10 = ; 4/10 = ; 8/10 = ; 20/100 = ;
> 50/100 =

Example 2: Write these decimal fractions as common fractions:

> 0.1 = ; 0.5 = ; 0.9 = ; 0.56 = ; 0.17 =

Hint: Remember to explain about place value and how it is that 0.1 is 1 tenth. Go back to using the column headings for place value to reinforce and make visual the concept.

THOUSANDS	HUNDREDS	TENS	UNITS	tenths	hundredths

Use the table to show that the tenth is less than one whole and that **10/10** *is* one whole (one unit).

IDEA 34

DECIMAL COMPUTATION

Use illustrations/visual aids/written figures which can be seen by all the children as you show them how to add and subtract decimal numbers. Make a habit of giving worked examples so that the children can see what is happening as you explain what it is you are doing. Check to make sure that all of the children can understand what you are illustrating.

Use the column headings (from Idea 30) within which to set out your figures and emphasize the significance of the decimal point as a 'separator' of the whole numbers from the parts of the whole numbers. Emphasize very strongly how important it is that the decimal points are all in line. Set out some basic computation for all children to see:

Example 1: 0.7 + 1.86 = **U.t h**

$$\begin{array}{r} 0.7\ 0 \\ +\ 1.8\ 6 \\ \hline 2.5\ 6 \\ \tiny{1} \end{array}$$

> add the *hundredths:* 0 + 6 = 6 *hundredths*
> then the *tenths:* 7 + 8 = 15 *tenths* which is
> 1 *Unit* and 5 *tenths*
> Carry the 1 unit from the 15 tenths (1 unit
> and 5 tenths) into the Units column and
> add to the existing Units to make 2
> units. The answer being 2.56.

Example 2: 7.92 – 3.567 = **U. t h**

$$\begin{array}{r} 7.9\ 2 \\ -\ 3.5\ 6 \\ \hline 4.3\ 6 \end{array}$$

Use the decomposition method:

1 To subtract the 6 hundredths from 2 hundredths you will need to decompose the 9 tenths.
2 Add one of the tenths to the 2 hundredths to make 12 hundredths.
3 Subtract 6 hundredths from the 12 hundredths to leave 6 hundredths.

4   Subtract 5 tenths from the **8** tenths (*remember you have decomposed the 9 tenths to leave 8 tenths*). This leaves 3 tenths.
5   Subtract 3 units from the 7 units. This leaves 4 units.

Set the children to work adding and subtracting decimals with some examples you make up or, better still, use the exercises from any textbook which you could buy, from some of the very many examples of primary numeracy which are now on sale in most bookshops. Direct the children to work quietly and on their own. Give the class about 20 minutes for about 10 examples of each operation, then go over the computation algorithms and the answers explaining and correcting as you go.

Look also at the examples I have given you in Idea 26.

I have always found children more eager to learn and enjoy any exercise which gives them the opportunity for practical work. One such exercise is graph work.

Example 1: Give the children the graph below which shows a number of words from a page, each of which is composed of a number of letters. Then set the questions below the graph:

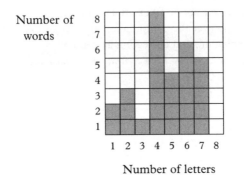

Number of words

Number of letters

¶ How many 4-letter words in the page?
¶ How many 1-letter words in the page?
¶ How many words on the page altogether?
¶ How many words on the page with 6 letters?
¶ Which was the most used numbers of letters?

Hint: This exercise is best presented on the board or OHT where you want whole-class participation.

Example 2: Get each child to make a graph of the frequency the letters of the alphabet occur in, say, four lines from their/a reading book. First explain how they should make a list of the letters of the alphabet then make a tally to record each time each letter appears in each line.

Show them what they should then do with their raw data. Explain how they will 'graph' these finding and make it clear about the axes of the graph. Illustrate this by drawing the axes on the board – horizontal axes for the letters of the alphabet and vertical axes representing frequency of appearance. Show the children how they will plot the frequency in number, against the letters of the alphabet. Make it clear how each division on the graph represents one letter or one appearance.

Hint: You could use other ideas such as mode of transport to school, children with pets, kinds of pets or numbers for school dinners . . .

IDEA 36

Use a pair of compasses to construct simple polygons in a circle. You will need to make sure the children know how to use compasses and a protractor.

Example 1: To construct a circle using compasses:

1 Explain how to set the compasses to a required measure.
2 Illustrate how to hold the compasses and the page/paper and describe a circle.

Hint: Give the children the practice of drawing at least three circles.

Example 2: To construct a polygon within a circle of 4cm radius:

1 Draw a circle of radius 4cm.
2 Extend a radius from the centre.
3 Determine the number of sides of the polygon you wish to construct, then divide this into 360 degrees.
4 Measure using the radii line to construct the found angle and mark off on the circumference.
5 Repeat for the number of sides.
6 Join the marks on the circumference to construct the polygon.

Hint: Make sure you have access to compasses and plenty of paper before you begin this exercise. Check that the children know how to use compasses and protractor – if not, then change the focus to teaching how to read the protractor. Should you discover that the children find this exercise too complex, just get them to learn to use the compasses and measure, drawing concentric circles from given radii or drawing interlocking circles of given radii on a straight line.

Teach the children to construct simple nets from dimensions you choose. Use nets of really simple shapes such as cubes or cuboids. You could prepare a simple worksheet on which you draw the net of a simple cube which the less able child could cut out and assemble.

The objective of this particular exercise will be to help the children to develop the skills of measuring using the ruler:

¶ working to a given plan
¶ drawing straight lines with pencil and ruler
¶ drawing and visualizing the plan of the 'net'
¶ using scissors to cut out the net
¶ constructing the three-dimensional shape from its 'net'

Hint: Make sure you have sufficient scissors and glues sticks for this work.

NETS OF CUBES AND CUBOIDS

THE PLENARY SESSION

Always conclude your numeracy session by:

¶ showing an example of a well-finished article
¶ going over what the children have done in the session in terms of measuring, planning, drawing, cutting and gluing
¶ reinforcing what has been learned – measure, shape, accuracy of cut and fit
¶ 'testing'/checking that the children have understood the work of the session
¶ getting the children to see what it is they have done in the session – what is the finished product? – what skills did they achieve from this work?
¶ getting the children calmed, reflective and focused before the end of the session.

Hint: Use a question-and-answer stage – for example you might get the children to say what they have learned, what they found, what they thought of what they learned, how they might remember what they had learned, did they have any difficulties and whether they found the work easier after the session.

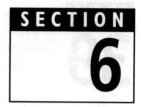

Science

Science is a lovely subject to teach and, like maths, can be great fun. The DfES site www.standards.dfes.gov.uk/schemes2 sets out a scheme of study for KS1 and KS2 but makes it plain that the scheme is not statutory and that the individual units may be combined with units from schemes for other subjects.

Primary schools tend in the main to follow the content outline set out by the DfES, which sets out the content for the 6 year groups of the primary school.

In all there are 38 units listed, from Unit 1 for Year 1 children, right up to Unit 6 for the children in Year 6. What I set out below is a summary of the main study areas:

- Living things: ourselves – plants and animals – respiration – movement – hygiene – health – feeding – habitat – variation
- Force and energy: electricity – sound – movement – friction – light
- Matter: classification – rocks and soil – changes in state – dissolving
- The solar system: sun, moon and earth

Hint: Check the DfES site for yourself and prepare the work which you might enjoy teaching and which you know might be the most likely to be well resourced – electricity, for example, and it is highly likely that every school will have a stock of bulbs, batteries, leads, crocodile clips and perhaps, buzzers and motors. At the other end of the spectrum, learning about living things will be the kind of subject which is least likely to require huge resources – what about a study of ourselves, food and digestion, health and hygiene, movement, respiration, sight and the senses for example? For your typical lesson you should aim to:

- Begin your lesson by asking the children what they think will happen if . . . I placed this against my magnet, dropped this, if I put this in, if I put this in front of, for example. This stage is particularly important because what you are doing is to have the children think and then generate hypotheses which you will go on to test.

- Once you have a majority response tell the class you will test to see if they were correct; ask the children to carry out their own tests to find out: what floats and what sinks, what carries electricity, what sorts of things are attracted to a magnet.
- Get the children to write what they did, to record their findings (what happened) and to write their conclusions (what they learned/found out).
- Have some of the children tell the class about their work and learning.
- Conclude the lesson by going over what it is that they learned in the session.

LIVING THINGS – OURSELVES

A good range of material can be used across almost the whole of the primary school through teaching about the human body and some of the areas you should be prepared to cover will be:

¶ parts of the body
¶ the skeleton
¶ the heart
¶ the senses
¶ the digestive system
¶ the circulatory system
¶ the respiratory system
¶ food, nutrition and diet

You may not need too much in the way of materials and equipment for these topic areas although I would advise that you have:

¶ lots of visual resources such as sufficient books for each child to be able to see the pictures/illustrations
¶ posters which are clearly visible from the back of the classroom
¶ models – the skeleton/eye/human body/plant
¶ worksheets and activity work for the children
¶ class/year group text/reference books
¶ videotapes/CD specific to the topic under study

Hint: Children learn best when they work from their own level of understanding and experience. Any new concepts will be more readily absorbed and assimilated by the child if he/she is able to make the links from their past learning to new learning experiences. When you teach the children about the human body, you should begin with what the children understand most – themselves. Get them to:

¶ look at their own hands/feet
¶ how they feel, touch (sense/sensing the world)
¶ how they see (senses)
¶ how they eat/taste (senses/digestion/dentition)
¶ what they eat (food/diet/build/exercise)
¶ how they move (body parts/locomotion/exercise)

- breathing (parts of the body/lungs/pulse/exercise/movement)
- heart beat (parts of the body/lungs/heart/pulse/exercise/movement)

This is one of the main topic areas where you can, with planning, deliver a really good lesson without the need for lots of equipment, materials and apparatus, using the children as your resources and getting them to observe, measure, examine, test and record.

The topic areas which could be the most interesting might include:

- plants – parts and function (roots/leaves/stem/flower/fruit)
- animals – classification – type/species (locomotion/breathing/breeding/feeding/habitat)
- interdependence of the various types/species (comparing/classification/ecological niche/adaptation)
- ecosystems (niche/habitat/adaptation)

You will need access to plants if you are to be able to have the children observe, examine and test for themselves. You should consider taking in some flowers and plants. Explore the environment of the school to see if there are any areas where plants are growing. Ask if there are any pot plants which you could use or if the school has a nature area to which you could take the children. Your objective is to have the children examining the plant closely so that they can see and recognize the main parts of the plant. Get the children to use hand lenses and to draw what they see. Teach them about how the leaves need sunlight to make food. Use the term photosynthesis with the Year 6 children about how in this process the leaves of the green plant take in carbon dioxide, which is then combined with water being sucked up by the roots to form the food the plant needs. Get the children to examine, draw and write notes about the root system of the plant – how its function is to anchor the plant and to absorb nutrients and moisture from the soil.

Hint 1: I found the Letts Educational publication on KS2 Science Revision notes particularly useful in providing work and ideas on the human body and on living things. You will find it quite rewarding to explore and examine the www.bbc.co.uk/schools site for additional and very useful material, ideas, lesson plans and interactive work. Check to see if the school has the Science Explorer program as this is also very good for ideas for teaching all of the KS2 subject areas in science and for interactive work and learning. Google has 10 pages of reference and resource ideas on KS1 and 2 science, or you could try www.edpax.com for interactive software on KS1 and 2 science.

Hint 2: If at all possible, make up a videotape/CD on the human body and splice in any programmes on plant growth and development which you can then take in to any primary school as your personal reserve material.

Before you begin this lesson on magnets you should make sure that you have sufficient magnets of different types – ring, horseshoe, button, ceramic or bar for example.

The main objective of the work on this topic would be to have the children test different materials to find out which will be attracted to the magnets and which will not. Pay particular attention to the development of appropriate vocabulary specific to this topic area; use correct terminology, such as metals, fabric, plastic, wood, attraction, repel, iron, aluminium, for example. You should have the children:

¶ collect a range of materials to test for attraction to a magnet
¶ classify the materials tested into different categories such as metals, wood, stone or fabrics, for example
¶ make hypotheses on what they think will happen before they make their tests and write up their observations
¶ test for polarity – forces of attraction and repulsion. How do different magnets respond to these forces – which are the working parts of the magnet (vocabulary: poles, attraction, repulsion)
¶ find out what magnets 'do' when placed near each other
¶ test to see if magnets work 'through' material. Place one magnet below the table and a paperclip or other iron object on the table above the magnet – move the magnet.
¶ make written conclusions of what they observed and learned. Get them to write and draw diagrams to record how they were able to find out that magnets only attract ferrous materials and how they found out which 'parts' of the magnet 'work'.

There are innumerable other experiments which can be carried out on magnets which you will find on the DfES standards site or on the google pages on KS1 and 2 science.

MATERIALS

The objective in teaching this topic is to have the children learn about the characteristics of materials. You will need to ensure that you have access to items such as wood, plastic, fabrics, metals, cork, polystyrene and stone, for example, which the children can see, feel, touch and work on. The main objective is to classify the materials as metals, plastics, textiles, woods and rocks (see table opposite).

You could then focus on experimenting to test for:

a   Hardness – use the scratch test. Ask the children what it is they need to make a mark on the material whether using their fingernail or a pin. Get them to test different materials such as slate, rubber, wood, plastic, brick, glass, metals and ceramics, to determine what is hard – whether it is like rubber or brittle like china or glass, or is it like rock or iron, or wood? Have the children make up a table of different materials against each of which they record the results of their experiment to test for hardness.

b   Test to see what materials are waterproof by pouring or dripping water on various materials such as wool, cotton, synthetic materials, metal foil, a plastic bag, a paper bag. What happens, does the water soak through?

c   Check materials for density – floating and sinking – use a bowl of water and immerse the object under study. Try stones, corks, wood blocks, plastic items, fabric pieces, rubber, glass mirror, plastic or metal objects.

d   Insulation – test to see if certain materials such as cotton, synthetic materials, egg boxes, cardboard boxes, metal foils, plastic bags are good at keeping/out heat/cold – stopping heat loss.

	Metals	Plastics	Textiles	Woods	Rocks
Examples	iron, gold, aluminium	polythene, polystyrene	cotton, wool	pine, beech, oak	granite, sandstone
Main features	makes a ringing sound when struck; cold to the touch; will conduct heat	easy to mould into complicated shapes when hot; warm to the touch; burns	easy to cut and make into sheets; very warm to the touch; burns	easy to saw and cut into shape; warm to the touch; burns	cold to the touch
Hardness	hard to the touch	usually quite soft	soft	hard	very hard
Strength	usually very strong	strong	some strong, some easily torn	strong	very strong
Where from	in the ground	man-made	animals and plants	trees	in the ground

63

IDEA 44

ELECTRICITY

Show the children how to make up simple circuits using a bulb, battery and two leads. Using this as the basic test circuit, have the children leave a gap in the circuit and have them test for:

a   Conductivity – get the children to find out what sorts of materials they can put into the gap to make the bulb light up – get them to classify the materials according to which ones will conduct electricity so the bulb in the circuit lights. Have the children use wooden or plastic rulers, class scissors or compasses, protractors, their pencil case, corks, stone or a piece of their personal jewellery to test for conductivity.

b   Insulators – what sorts of materials can they put into the gap in their electrical circuit which will *not* make the bulb light up. Have them classify the insulators. They should use fabrics, plastic rulers, cork, glass mirror, rubber, pencils, pens to test as insulators.

c   Using electrical energy, have the children try building different kinds of circuits incorporating buzzers, bells and bulbs – they should place these objects in the electrical circuit. Have them make up their circuit, then connect the buzzer bell or bulb in the gap.

d   Try building series and parallel circuits – one is like the Christmas tree lights (one off, all off) – the other is like the house lights (one off, the rest are there to let you know which one is off!). Have the children connect the battery to a succession of bulbs in a daisy-chain with the last bulb being connected to the battery for the series circuit. Connect each bulb to both poles of the battery with successive bulbs connected to the contacts of each preceding bulb to form your parallel circuit. Have the children make conclusions for the difference in brightness. Remove a bulb from each of the circuits, observe the effect and explain in conclusions.

Use a torch, the sun, the OHP to illustrate to the children how:

¶ Light can be seen to travel in straight lines – show them how to prove this.
¶ Ask them to test to see if light can be seen around corners.
¶ Ask them to find out if shadows have clear 'edges'.
¶ Use the light source but have the children sit side-on to the source so the beam is at right angles to the class. Can they see the light? Point the torch toward the class – can they see the light? Create a shadow – does it have clean edges?
¶ Help the children to explore how shadows are formed – have them discover where the light source has to be for the shadow to form – have the children draw diagrams and explain how they have formed shadows using torches, the overhead projector, lights in the classroom or the sun in the playground.
¶ Teach the class about objects which are opaque, translucent and transparent. Get them to find out what happens if they interpose a book, a piece of clear plastic or glass in front of the light source – get them to write what happens. Have them look at the fluorescent light cover in the classroom – this is translucent – ask them, what does it do? How do they think it works? Whether it stops the light. Ask if they think it spreads/diffuses the light.
¶ Have the children explore reflections in mirrors and shiny surfaces. Direct them to hold a matt covered book in a beam of light. They should then try the same test using a mirror or shiny plastic or opaque/matt plastic or sugar paper, for example, then get them to write and draw diagrams to show and write about their findings.
¶ Get the children to examine what happens when they hold a hand lens up to the window so that the image falls onto a piece of paper. Get them to focus the image so that it becomes clear. They will see the image of the window upside down. Ask them to write a hypothesis as to how this has happened.

- If you have any available, give the children some lenses – concave and convex, bi-concave and bi-convex – ask them to find out what do they do as they look through these lenses. They could then be instructed to place a lens in front of the torch/light source to see what happens. Fill a clear glass jar with water and get the children to look at the print on a page through the jar. Get them to write to explain what happens. Give the children a Petri dish or a transparent plastic ink cartridge box on a page of print then ask them to add one single drop of water onto the dish or container and ask them to look at what it does to the print. (The water drop will act as a lens.)
- Have the children make a periscope using mirrors. Ask them to write about how they think this works. Aim to have them work out that the image they see is reflected by one angled mirror onto the other angled mirror and then into the eye.
- Have the children examine their partner's eye – get them to draw what they see. Show them a model or poster of the eye and its parts and get them to write notes on how they work.
- Have the children examine their partner's eye under the classroom light. Have them write and draw what they see when the light is striking the eye. Get them to place a book as a shield to shade the eye from the light source. Have them look closely to see what happens when the eye is in the light and what happens when it is shaded from the light. Get them to write and draw what they have seen.
- As an independent exercise you should get the children to write how they think we see. Get them to think about whether the light goes out from the eye, or does the light come off an object into the eye? Ask them to think about why we cannot see when there is no light.

It might be a good idea for you to conduct demonstration lessons for the following ideas. Gather the children, either as a class group or individual table groups around the apparatus/demonstration table and carry out the tests yourself. Make sure you involve the children by asking for comments, ideas, thoughts, solutions or reasons. Test:

¶ the upthrust of buoyancy – floating and sinking – test to see what floats and what sinks and think why – mass/density. Use the class sink or a plastic tank and test to see what type of objects will float and which will sink. Use a wood and a plastic ruler, rubber, pencil, biro, scissors, compasses, for example. Generate hypotheses on what the force is which causes the object to sink. Or ask what the force is which causes the object to float. Try an inflated balloon in the water!

¶ the pull of gravity – weight/mass. Ask such questions as: Why do 'things' fall to earth? Do all 'things' fall at the same rate? Why does a sheet of paper 'float' to earth? Does the air act as a cushion for all 'things'?

¶ push and pull – resistance to movement – friction and lubrication. Ask the children how easy they think it would be to push heavy objects such as a cupboard or a car. Get them to try pushing a gram mass on a smooth surface then on a piece of glass, paper, or the carpet. Have them write their thoughts about what happened. Get them to try pushing the same gram mass over a surface using pencils as rollers. Ask them to think about why it is harder to push a gram mass on a rough surface than on a smooth surface; what they think putting water onto a surface will do – will it make the surface slippery? Will oil make the surface more slippery than water? Then test/demonstrate their hypotheses.

¶ levers and pulleys – demonstrate how they work as multipliers of force to reduce energy input. Get one of the children to try lifting a library book (hard back) with one finger. You should then insert the end of a pencil under the book with a rubber or another pencil as a pivot before you press down on the lever (pencil) with one finger ask the children what they think will happen. If the school has any pulleys, show the children how pulling against gravity using a pulley is much easier than lifting against gravity. (You will need a convenient brace from which to suspend your pulley.)

¶ forces in equilibrium – that is if the forces are balanced there is no movement – demonstrate this by showing that a book sitting on a table has potential energy. Prove this as you push the book off the table and the energy is released – gravity is acting on the book while the table arrested the movement of the book to earth. Demonstrate using a tank of water or a beaker that a boat/buoyant object floats because the pull of gravity and the push of buoyancy is equal.

These topic areas are enormous and you will find separate books with many ideas on how to teach any one of the above topics.

Should you find that you have little or no apparatus or materials, you could undertake a lesson on classification and the characteristics of matter. Have the children fill in a table, such as:

Solid	Liquid	Gas
Ice	Perfume	Oxygen

Ask the children to think about some other examples of solids, liquids and gases which they could add to the table. The follow-on for this exercise would be for the children to make up a table of their own to list the characteristics of matter, such as:

Solid	Liquid	Gas
Size, shape and mass and can be measured easily	Size, mass but no shape of its own. Can be measured easily	No size, no shape and no mass – fills any space – can be squashed

You could guide the children by asking them to think about observable characteristics then get them to write explaining how:

water can become a solid – *freezing*

they can smell perfume or vinegar when it is a liquid – *evaporation*

water vapour can become a liquid – *condensing*

gas can be squashed – *pressure* as in being squashed into a balloon

One of the most common topics to appear in the science SATs tests has been that which featured questions and diagrams related to the solar system. This can be one of the most fascinating and rewarding topics and will require very little in the way of elaborate resources. At most you will need to make up a worksheet that you can add to your personal resource bank that will teach some of the basic facts about our solar system. Basically you will need one worksheet with a clear diagram of our solar system with the sun and the planets in order or orbit. This worksheet should be supplemented by another worksheet with facts about our solar system:

FACTS ABOUT THE SUN

¶ the sun is over one million kilometres in diameter
¶ it is a star
¶ it is a source of heat and light
¶ the sun is at the centre of our solar system.

FACTS ABOUT THE EARTH

¶ it is a planet of the sun
¶ it is a ball of rock, water and gas
¶ it is 12,762 kilometres in diameter
¶ it does not produce light
¶ it orbits the sun

FACTS ABOUT THE MOON

¶ it is a ball of rock 3,450 kilometres in diameter
¶ it is a satellite of the earth – orbiting the earth
¶ it does not emit but reflects sunlight

Other planets – have the children carry out their own research using the library or the Internet to find out

¶ what these other planets are – rock, gas or other
¶ how many of them there are in our solar system
¶ their positions in the solar system
¶ whether they have any satellites of their own.

Get the children to work in project form so that they write whatever they can find out by themselves and they should enhance their project work with pictures or diagrams or drawings of the solar system. Individuals can then be encouraged to give a talk to the class or in assembly on their work.

IDEA

49

What I would recommend is that you have a good demonstration introduction which you will use to stimulate interest. Tell the children what you intend to do, then get them to make a hypothesis as to what will happen before you start; then get them to talk about what they have seen and how they rationalize what they have seen, and how close they were to guessing what did happen. Take magnets, for example: tell the children that you intend to find out what will 'stick to' or be attracted to a magnet. Use their terminology first, then give them the correct vocabulary to use in its place. Once the children have made their hypotheses, test the magnet on different materials without explaining anything. Stimulate thought into who was right – then go on to ask why some materials are attracted to the magnet; why some others are not? How to classify these materials; which ends of the magnet are attractive? Why not other parts? Get the children to do lots of testing and drawing and, if they are capable, writing their findings/thoughts/ explanations.

Use this kind of format for lessons on any of the other topic areas I have suggested.

Hint: You should make sure to check out the school resources for whatever apparatus, equipment and materials you can lay your hands on. Use the school's ICT software and the Internet; check to see if you could be fitted into the ICT suite timetable.

SECTION 7

Design technology/ craft

The process will be to get the children to make topical cards on a theme such as Easter, Christmas, birthdays, get well, holiday, greetings, congratulations, moving house or postcards.

Give the children a couple of ideas as a starter – have a couple of examples of commercial cards which you can show them, then get them to use their own imagination to *create* ideas of their own. Encourage them to be as freely creative as they can because you are looking for something original – their own idea.

Have the children make a design of their ideas on paper first – scrap paper will do so that they can explore, create and make their mistakes. An additional idea would be for the children to use IT to produce their designs. When they, and you, are satisfied, have them develop the idea, working from their template on card, sugar paper or good-quality material. The cards should aim to contain a neatly written message and could be decorated using paints, felt-tip pens or glue and glitter dusts.

The idea is to end up with a small card marker bearing a name finished in felt, paint or glitter glue which can serve as a place saver on a table setting.

Begin by having the children draw a rectangle of 8cm by 3cm then get them to explore writing their own names in fancy scripts within this rectangle. Once the children are satisfied with their choice of script, have them work on the final design on card. Get them to draw, then cut out one rectangle 8cm by 6cm on the card, which should then be scored and folded over to form two rectangles, 8cm by 3cm. Have them now write their chosen place names in their selected script using paints, felt-tip pens or the special glitter glue pens. The finished article could then be put on display for the class teacher to admire before they take the work home.

MAKE SIMPLE TABLE PLACE SAVERS

¶ Design, make and decorate a bookmark. Cut a number of strips of card/sugar paper 21cm long and 4cm wide. Have the children make some design/decoration on this strip so that one end of the longer side will stand proud of the book page to show the design and act as a bookmark. They can either use their initials or make a little drawing, or write a slogan which they should then decorate using paints, felt-tip pens or the glitter glue pens which produce a very pretty effect.

¶ Design and make a name badge/logo using your initials. Explain to the children that you want them to design a badge using their own initials, which will look like the school badge or the badge of a football club. They make their designs of a shield/shape outline on scrap paper then add their initials inside the shape/shield. When they and you are satisfied with the designs, have them copy the design on card, if you can get it, or on light-coloured sugar paper. The children should then decorate their initials using paints, felt-tip pens or the glitter glue pens, cut out the design shape and stick it on a safety pin using sticky tape so the children can wear their 'badge' home.

This is a good opportunity for you to enthuse the children to be really creative. Talk to them about how many a book will draw attention because of its attractive, arresting and imaginative dust jacket. Illustrate your point by showing the children some designs which you consider attractive using copies of books aimed at their age range, explaining what it is you like about the cover in particular. Ask the children what attracts them to choosing a book from the library. Tell them then that you want them to design and decorate a book jacket of their own, and the subject of the book can be anything – adventure, science fiction, mythological beings, magic, fantasy, wizardry, medieval romanticism or whatever they care to choose. Get them to plan their design in rough then onto clean A4 paper, which should represent the front and back of the book jacket. Get them to add colour using paints, felt-tip pens or whatever they think they need to make the design eye-catching or atmospheric. The finished product can then be pinned on any free board for display.

Hint: Look over the room or the area in which you are expected to teach this subject. Check out for possible hazards, potentially dangerous materials or implements such as Stanley knives or craft knives, tools of any sort or liquids, for example. Do what you can to obviate any accidents or incidents.

Check also to ensure that you are able to access whatever materials you will need for the session. You could also check out the DfES standards site at www.dfes.standards.gov.uk/schemes2 for further examples of ideas which can be used to enhance your teaching.

DESIGNING A BOOK COVER

Art

IDEA

54

LINE DRAWING

Have the children draw an outline of:

¶ their own hand
¶ their training shoe
¶ their school shoe
¶ their pencil case/box
¶ their desk (tidy) or any desk furniture.

I have found this session to be a good introduction to drawing, especially if you begin by asking the children to trace around their subject and, having achieved the outline, get them to 'fill in' the details. It is very useful to have the whole class drawing the same subject because you will be able to get them to make suggestions, cross-fertilize ideas, work on techniques and share successes to avoid failures or pitfalls. You could also use some of the work as examples to stimulate those bereft of ideas. As part of the techniques, the children should be guided into how they could represent shadows, lines, characteristics, details and shading on the subject. Tell them that you expect they will need more than one attempt before they can achieve what they think they like and that they can work until they get their idea right.

I have found that the most common thing about art is that children are hugely self-critical and, with few exceptions, will claim to be 'useless at art', using this as a reason for not working. What the children need is support in developing the beginnings of self-confidence. Sometimes children need to be reassured that they are not expected to be good at their first attempt, but with practice they will improve, and that they should try and keep trying until they are happy with what they have done.

What you must do is to reassure them by being supportive, positive and constructively critical – show them how to improve.

The older or more able children could be expected to try drawing using a less directed approach. You could, for example:

¶ direct the children to draw a three-dimensional representation of their reading book or a textbook
¶ ask the children to design a dust jacket for a fictional story – you will have to make up a title for them
¶ get the children to observe and draw a window in the classroom and to include and draw the view from that window
¶ have the children observe and make a representational drawing of a friend or their class teacher
¶ encourage the children to make a design of their dream car or house.

Hint: Make sure that you emphasize that you want them to draw *their* teacher and *not* you, this could invite wild, provocative caricatures of yourself which will cause much disruption. You could tell the children that you want to see whether they can represent their teacher from memory alone. Talk first – enthuse and encourage so that you actually get the children in the mood to be creative.

I have tried all of these starting points and have found that, by working from the outline drawing, the children then have their parameters within which to become more expressive. Having drawn the outline, the children must be encouraged to fill in the details, adding shading, lines, characteristics and details as they see them.

FREE DRAWING

It has been my experience that children love painting. The very thought of water, paints, brushes, the aprons and newspapers on the table seems to be the stimulus which generates excitement until it comes to actually creating. The secret is to give the children clear instructions on what is expected of them and the end product must be within their eidetic imaging so that they can actually visualize what it is they are aiming to create. Some ideas you might apply to stimulate painting could be:

- 'free' paint a three-colour spiral beginning at the centre of the page. Start with one colour spiralling gently to the perimeter of the page and within this spiral add the other two colours following the first spiral. The children should then try to blur the edges of the three colours
- using two strong colours begin by making bold vertical strokes of paint at opposite ends of the paper mixing and merging the colours as they meet in the centre of the page
- paint a representation of the face of a clown
- paint a representation of a flower or bunch of flowers
- paint a design of a CD cover.

Note that the objective of this session will be for the children to learn to use paint freely, without the constraint of having to capture likeness, expressing themselves to their own ability. Reassure and remind them that you want to see as many different paintings as there are people in the class. You don't want to see work being copied and that all painting should be individual efforts created over time and with care.

Teach them to plan their work, making a light pencil drawing on the paper before thinking of paint. They should then think about the colours they want to use before they begin mixing colour. Get them to visualize the picture on the paper so that they use the whole of their 'canvas' to produce an attractive finished picture without leaving any blank border spaces. Give the children some examples using pictures as a visual stimulus to illustrate what it is you are aiming for them to achieve.

I find this session very exciting since children can be really expressive without being inhibited either by their ability to draw, by having to commit paint to paper or by having a huge white space to fill. What enthuses the children is to work on *black* sugar paper, using chalks to make bold lines, fine lines, shading and blending, building up on the background rather than filling in, to produce an almost three-dimensional effect of colour, which stands out on the black paper.

Begin by giving them a word picture – make it up, where you describe your own experience of a fireworks scene or a snow scene, or show them a picture, a postcard or use a book or the Internet, anything which gives them a visual cue as to what it is they should be aiming to capture. The stimulus you should try may be to describe:

¶ a fireworks scene – colours, explosion, light and atmosphere
¶ a log fire – form, colours, heat, light, cool areas and atmosphere
¶ a snow-covered tree – textures, grain and a dusting of snow
¶ a rural snow-covered scene
¶ a swallowtail butterfly.

Note: The objective of this form of art work will be to give the children the experience of experimenting with coloured chalks on black sugar paper adding details, as a contrast to beginning with a sheet of white paper which they should then 'fill-in'.

Hints:

1 Set the parameters at the start of the lesson so that you control the use materials, colours and techniques, because with the emphasis on freedom of expression some children will want to widen their access to materials and this could be untidy, unstructured and potentially disruptive as more and more children begin to follow suit. There are, however, those children who will simply give you the minimum because they can do no more.

2 Make sure you have a really good idea of the resources available to you either in the classroom or at least to hand and easily accessible, so that you have *everything* to hand before you begin your lesson.

3 You should also make sure that you give the children a task they can complete and that you have some additional work for the early finishers.

4 I would advise that in addition to beginning your session with *everything* that you will need you will also have arranged the work space to suit the activity you have planned. Make sure that after the session you will leave the room as tidy as, or tidier than, before you began.

5 One essential tip is to close the session 15 minutes before the scheduled end so that you can clear up, clean up and have a closure activity for the children to show and talk about their work.

History

IDEA

58

The history scheme set for the primary school by the DfES is not statutory and is presented in individual units. The units are aimed at pupils who are attaining at levels broadly appropriate for their age and may therefore be adapted to meet pupil needs and it is also suggested that the units may be combined with units for other subjects. The DfES lists 20 units for KS1 and KS2, and what I list here is an encapsulation of the main themes:

- Comparing past and present – rich and poor – how life has changed – Britain since the 1930s – World War II
- The Romans
- The Anglo-Saxons
- The Vikings
- Ancient Egyptians
- The Greeks
- The Victorians
- The Tudors – Henry VIII
- The life of a famous person – e.g. Florence Nightingale or Winston Churchill

You will find that the history is therefore taught in discrete topics for each of the year groups taking the form of projects and it is likely that the class teacher will reschedule the lesson rather than expect you to teach the lesson. However, that is not to say that you will not be asked to teach to the material left for you by the class teacher. As a result of this, it is difficult to prepare for, to teach or to cover this subject but it is always wise to be prepared with your own material and resources, should you find yourself having to teach history.

Essentials of your standard resources pack should be a videotape or an audiotape with a historical content such as *The Machine Gunners*, *Goodnight Mr Tom*, or any topic on the Victorians or whatever you might find stocked in the primary education section of a good bookstore. Study the subject matter in the list of units I have given you and you might perhaps be able to teach to one topic area which you might have covered yourself and which you might enjoy.

- Begin with a discussion on the nature of history. Get the children to articulate their thoughts about history. Explore and encourage any thoughts on history as a construct of past events recorded from recollections, hearsay, word of mouth, written records, art, artefacts, buildings, customs, laws and rules.
- Guide the discussion and examination of the sources of history paying particular attention to the distinction between primary and secondary sources and how children should test for historical accuracy and veracity over hearsay and embellishment of accounts.
- Examine other concepts of history recorded from word of mouth stories and accounts. The Bible, for example, or other holy books which are the written accounts of observers or at best second-hand recollections.
- Keep the discussion on track and then get the children to write their ideas, perhaps under the title of 'What I think history is . . .'

IDEA 60

If you have been left a prepared, planned session you may find that you will have been left audiotapes, videotapes or CDs which focus on the content of the session. Check that you are familiar with the hardware necessary to use this material and ask the children to make notes of what it is they may see and hear which will give them some notion of what may be historical content.

Have the children examine the accuracy of what may be dramatic creation and how much factual account. Get them to consider whether what they have seen and heard may be factual, and whether it can be tested as being based on fact and how it might be tested for authenticity and accuracy.

Determine what appear to be the key issues which the material is exploring – is it the clothes, the way of life, how people talked, what they did, how they lived?

Have the children compare the past with the present and discuss, then make a written account of what they have learned. They will need the audio/video material as a reference point.

Have the children examine what was portrayed as the past and how the same factors in the present may be compared and related and have them write their perceptions of change or the comparisons they feel able to make.

The school ICT suite or Internet are also very valuable resources and should be used wherever possible. There is a very wide range of very good resource material available both online and on school-based software.

¶ Check out the school ICT suite and assess whether and when you could take the class in for their history session. Make use of the Internet and whatever software/Internet sites you may know yourself. Check out the sites and make notes on what is available.

¶ Spend some time examining the school-based history software to get some ideas of what is available to you in the school as you may be able to use the class computers if you are unable to use the ICT suite.

Hint: The BBC history homepage is particularly good for its interactive pages. You can visit any page designed specifically for a period in time and the children can interact by, for example, going undercover to see what life was like in Scotland in 1914, or take part in the world of Ancient Rome, or find out about how the children of the Vikings lived. You could also visit www.immersiveeducation.com and have the children enjoy another interactive site where, for example, the child is invited to type a response/comment in a speech bubble on screen and continue a dialogue with the historical characters – I tried one with Henry VIII!

USING ICT IN HISTORY

MAKING HISTORY NEWS

Examine the history pages on the Internet yourself before you apply them in the classroom to ensure that you are familiar with the material and so that you are fully aware of exactly what is available. Explore these pages carefully and claim some of it for your own applications by extending the use of the material. I used the idea of having the children write a story with the interview they had had with Henry VIII asking him about some of the decisions he had made regarding the building of the navy, or his prowess as a tennis player or other issues of his reign, for example. The horizon from this particular starting point is almost limitless in that, for example, you could have the children writing about the Roman sentries on Hadrian's Wall, or their settlement at Fishborne Palace in AD 575. The children should write their interviews from a factual basis using the results of their research on the Internet.

Hint: It is highly likely that if you are left work to cover in history you are bound to find that you will also be left the resources with which to teach the planned content. But nevertheless always be prepared just in case the cover is unplanned. I have experienced just such a need on a number of occasions.

Geography

TEACHING GEOGRAPHY

The DfES lists 25 units (www.standards.dfes.gov.uk/
schemes2) for the children of KS1 and 2, and I have
done my own combining and summarizing as follows:

- our local area – investigating – the school – us in
  our local environment – traffic – our own area –
  improvements – conservation – the news – activities
  in life
- an island home
- weather
- villages
- Llandudno – Tocuaro – India – contrast of locality –
  global eye
- coasts
- rivers
- mountains
- the media – the news

I found it very useful to have a file with a resource bank
of worksheets before I started working as a supply
teacher. This resource file was particularly valuable
because I was able to concentrate on the teaching
without worrying about my resources.

Begin by explaining about how rainfall could collect, running off at the lowest point giving rise to rivulets, streams and rivers. Go over the stages of the life of the river using diagrams which you could draw either on the board or on a handout. Go to www.nationalgeographic. com/geographyaction/rivers, where you will find a mass of information on river formation together with interactive exercises that you could sift to get the information which you could use to enhance your lesson. You should explain:

¶ the life of a river from its youthful stage, as the speed and power of the water erodes the bed, cutting the 'v'-shaped valley and moving materials
¶ the mature and old age stages, and show how the speed of flow decreases while the mass increases contributing to meanders and the formation of oxbow lakes as the rivers mature
¶ how the water eventually flows out to sea at the mouth
¶ estuaries and the eventual deposition of material.

The worksheets on the BBC schools website on rivers are quite good, and you could save yourself a lot of time and effort by looking at these to make up your own. Have the children to make notes and diagrams or have them work from the worksheets you develop. The children could then undertake an exercise using a map of Great Britain, to find five rivers, tracing their source to their eventual entry into the sea.

MOUNTAINS

Explore the phenomena of hill and mountain formation. Don't expect to go into this too deeply because the concept of plate tectonics is a shade too abstract for the children of this age. However, you could simply explain that the mountains are formed when the earth's crust crumples – show them how this could occur as you push two jumpers or two open books against each other. The children could make notes or work from worksheets which you prepare on this topic. You could get them to use a map of Great Britain to find and identify the location of the Cheviots, Pennines, Ben Nevis, Snowdonia or the Grampians for example. You might consider going further afield, using the world atlas to find Everest, Mont Blanc, Mount Cameron, or K'ula Shan to further extend the children's knowledge of world locations.

The topic on volcanoes is a particularly rewarding area because the children do love the notions of the power and violence of the earth. You will need to explain about the crust of the earth and the plates. Think about the 'skin' left on cooling custard or the gravy from the Sunday roast. Below the 'solid skin' (crust) lies the molten/liquid body. Tell how the movement of the mantle causes the plates of the crust to move and how the weak points allow molten magma to surface. Cover the different types of volcano, such as those which lie along the edges of plates or those above the 'hot spots' far from plate edges. Explore the explosive or intermediate volcanoes with their characteristic cone shape, sometimes erupting explosively, and contrast this with the quiet volcanoes and their flattened shield shape, and how the magma rises from chambers. You would find it most useful if you were to prepare a set of worksheets before you begin teaching to use as handouts, so that you can have the children taking notes and completing your worksheets. The main idea on the worksheets should be to present the idea in diagrammatic form, what the volcano is and how the outer visible parts are caused by the reservoir of molten material below the surface. The exercises the children could then go on to would be to use the world atlas to find six volcanoes, three along the plate edges such as Mauna Loa and Kilauea and three others which are not on the fault lines.

A very good exercise to complement and enhance skills in using the atlas would be for the children to use the index pages of the atlas to find, for example, countries, cities, seas or oceans. Generate a worksheet of an outline of the world that you keep in your resource folder, which you can copy for each child to complete in the atlas exercise. The object of the exercise is for the children to learn to use the atlas index to find location which they should then mark on to their map worksheet and in so doing they will reinforce their knowledge for future reference. You could set them to find, for example:

¶ Canada, Italy, Turkey, Chile, Argentina or Norway
¶ Quebec, San Francisco, Tokyo, Athens, Reykjavik or Delhi
¶ The Indian Ocean, Arctic Ocean, Mediterranean Sea, Caspian Sea or North Sea.

Hint: For good effective, stress-free teaching I would advise that:

¶ Before you start your teaching you should research the primary education section of the local bookstores to give you some insight into the areas being covered by the children in the primary school.
¶ Check out the school ICT suite and assess whether and when you could take the class in for their geography session. Make use of the Internet and whatever software/Internet sites you may know yourself. Check out the sites and make notes on what is available.
¶ Spend some time examining the school-based geography software to get some ideas on what is available to you in the school as you may be able to use the class computers if you are unable to use the ICT suite.
¶ It is always useful to have, in support, a videotape/CD of a programme on volcanoes, or *The Blue Planet*, or rivers, or Globe Explorer, for example, which you can use in the event that you are not left any material or should the work left be inadequate for the time set for the session.

¶ Make some time to check the school and classroom resources and the fiction library for class copies of history textbooks. Look out especially for the history/geography boxes which are dedicated to specific topics as these comprise a complete 'kit' of topic-specific resources which will include audio and videotapes, books, artefacts and teaching notes.

RE

IDEA

68

TEACHING RE

A locally agreed syllabus for RE at KS2 is posted on the DfES standards site and, although not statutory, is generally used by the primary schools and is laid out in units beginning with 3 units for the reception class, and thereafter with multiple units for each of the successive year groups. The areas covered are the main tenets and characteristics of the Christian, Jewish, Hindu and Muslim faiths and their main festivals.

I suggest that you take in a story that you know to have overtly moral content which can be used to have the children discussing and then writing or drawing their own thinking from this stimulus. You could use, for example, the story of the Pied Piper of Hamelin. Read or tell the story to the class, then ask the children what they think about the story; do they see any relevance to us for today? What are the implications for us today? Can they translate the story to modern times? The idea of honesty and keeping to a bargain or to one's word should be the central focus, and then of course the implications of failing to fulfil commitments made.

Those stories which do not overtly feature Jesus Christ as a central feature are always good for their moral content and can be used safely without fear of causing offence to children of other faiths. Some ideas you could use might be:

¶ Use the story of the Tower of Babel and have the children focus on the idea of 'mankind' developing notions of omnipotence in making efforts to visit God in his kingdom.

¶ The Good Samaritan – neighbourliness/the love for a fellow man.

¶ The Prodigal Son – this particular tale has many facets: the forgiveness by the parent, the dawning of realization by the son that what he had was better than he had at first thought, and the misunderstanding and bitterness of the son who stayed at home and who felt alienated/cheated.

You could use some of the teachings of Jesus as Prophet to stimulate thought into how relevant these teachings are to life today. Look for example, at:

¶ Casting the first stone – this is the story where Jesus invited those without sin to be the first to stone the 'sinner'. The moral line here of course is for us not to make judgements and lay condemnation when we ourselves may have our own failings. This story has echoes in the saying 'one should be aware of the plank in ones own eye while examining the splinter in the eye of another'. Have the children examine these stories for the moral and to focus on how they might be effective in their own world in the twenty-first century.

¶ There is the story of the curing of the 10 lepers, where Jesus cures the lepers and all go on their way rejoicing but only one comes back to thank him for being cured. Explore the humanity of showing gratitude and thanks. Have the children had any instances of where they too may have experienced such a lack of recognition of compassion, humanity, favour? Get them to discuss and to write their own feelings and thoughts.

It is always a good idea to have in your resource kit a book on assembly stories. These can easily be adapted for an RE lesson so that you read the story and discuss the implications, the message and then have the children explore the issues articulating their own points of view. A good example is the story of the Sword of Damocles – where the commoner expresses his envy of the king and is then invited to the banquet where he sits all evening under the sword suspended above him on a single hair. The moral being that we are never aware of the privations or the pressures of others whom we might envy for their lifestyle. Discuss with the children how this could be translated to their experience. Do some of them feel that the Queen or pop stars have a privileged position, for example? Get them to think very carefully about whether they feel that there are any disadvantages to being famous, and any advantages to their own situations. Keep the discussion limited to about 15 minutes, then get them to write their thoughts and conclusions.

Ask the class if there is anyone who is a Muslim, Jew, Hindu or belongs to any other old world religion. Be specific about this last category because the children might hijack the lesson by being provocative. An example of this arose out of my observation of a student taking such a lesson, who made the mistake of allowing a child to tell the class about how he believed in aliens. This then led other children into volunteering a whole range of beliefs including one who said that she believed her sister was an 'antagonistic'.

Having controlled the responses, ask the child to explain to the class about their beliefs and the main characteristics of their religion. You should then lead a short discussion to examine the differences between this religion and the main characteristics of Christianity or Hinduism or Islam. The objective of this exercise is to have the children explore the generic aspects of beliefs and practices. Where does it all stem from and what are the differences and similarities in prayer, in feasting and fasting? Are there special rules on dress – either for everyday or for services – for example? Use the children to give you the stimulus from which you can then have the class compare and contrast similarities and differences. The written work you should expect will be the children expressing what they have learned about different religions, about tolerance, about understanding of points of view and about beliefs and customs.

DIFFERENT FAITHS

IDEA 72

BELIEFS AND FAITH

Explore the idea of belief. Ask the children what they think the basis of a belief might be and in what they might believe. Ask for example:

- what are the beliefs?
- what are the characteristics – blind faith – trust – questioning?
- what are the commandments/tenets/rules?

Discuss and talk about how it is that we might have an unshakeable belief in the doctrine of, for example, global warming or political rhetoric, or the infallibility of religious doctrine. Explore the issues which cause young people to develop strong feelings of intolerance under the influence of religious indoctrination and then get the children to write their own thinking, beliefs and rationalization.

Almost all children will have heard of the Bible. Some will almost certainly have no knowledge, other than that it is a book. Find out if there is a copy in the classroom or the school and use it to have the class explore:

¶ What is it? (a recorded history of the writings and teachings of Christianity)
¶ Who uses it? (virtually every Christian has access to a copy – used by Ministers)
¶ When is it used? (used in services – used when people want to read and learn about the teachings of Christ)
¶ Why is it used? (to learn about the past, about the religion – some people feel good when they read about the teachings)

THE BIBLE

The objective will be for you to teach the children about recorded history of religions using the Torah and the Qur'an as further examples and determining how peoples of other faiths might have recorded their own beliefs. Ask if any children use or know of the Torah and Qu'ran and get them to explain what, who, when and why, as a comparison with the use of the Bible. If you can get hold of a copy, or better still a class set, of the Bible, look at the stories, the teachings and try to explore the writers and when they might have written, for example, the letters which form part of the Bible. Ask the children how they could find out more about these religious books – use the Internet to make your investigations. It would be really effective if you were able to get your own copy of the Qur'an or the Torah so that you could show the children the examples of the Holy Books.

RELIGIOUS BUILDINGS

This is a lovely topic because it has the effect of making religion and religious practices more concrete. Askjeeves.co.uk will provide you with a really good interactive session where you will see parts of religious buildings on screen and then you can ask the children to design their own place of worship. Having explored this site first, discuss with the children the purpose and function of places of worship. Focus on the similarities between Muslims and Jews in terms of segregating the male and female worshippers in their mosques and synagogues. Compare this with Christians who do not have this segregation. Have the children use the Internet to look at the architecture and layout of the interior of these buildings. If you have access to the RE resources on religious buildings, focus on the bold structures of the Christian Church, aspiring to be the house of God with its tower/steeple and bells. Compare this with the mosque, with its simple structure but characteristic minaret for the muezzin to call the faithful to prayer. Find out about how the synagogue might be different, yet share some aspects as plainness of structure, use and application with the mosque. Look at the differences in the furniture and significant focal points in each of these three buildings – find out their meanings and uses. If available, use the information in the class textbooks or the Internet on religious buildings.

Choose a religious festival such as Easter or harvest, Christmas, Eid or Diwali and get the children to discuss what they know and think about the chosen festival. Have the children then find out, using ICT and the Internet, the history, practices, customs and meanings of these festivals. Get the children to find out:

¶ The meanings of the festival – what does it represent – why is it of significance?
¶ What are the special points about this festival – the birth of Christ – the festival of light?
¶ What do people do at this time? (give presents, give to the poor, go to services)
¶ Are there special clothes to wear, foods to eat, things to do?

Lead the children to discuss, write and illustrate their findings. You could use 'picture' worksheets of the sort you will find in the Study Guide to Sikhism, Christianity, Judaism, Islam and Hinduism, for example.

RELIGIOUS FESTIVALS

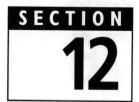

Information and communications technology

TEACHING ICT

Give the children the opportunity to undertake focused research out of which they should produce a handwritten report by, for example, using the Internet to find specific instructions. You could have the children find:

⁋ a recipe for home-made lemonade
⁋ how to roast chicken with garlic and parmesan
⁋ how to grow bedding plants such as *Nicotiana* or *doronicum*
⁋ how to set climbing plants such as *Akebia quinata* or the flame creeper *Tropaeolum speciosum*

or you can, of course, choose different examples those I have offered. The children should be expected to produce a manuscript report rather than printed copy because it is all too easy for them to find the page, download and then print information. The main object is for them to navigate the net, find the information, think about what parts of the information are relevant, be selective of what notes they will make and then produce the report in précis using their own words.

You will need a stimulus of some sort – a story which may be topical or something related to what the children are experiencing, but which can be sensationalized. Take the weather for example; start off with a discussion of the weather of that day or the past week and how conditions might develop to indicate global warming of our planet. The children should then be expected to go on to write an article warning about how the weather is changing so gradually but significantly and our leaders are too preoccupied with the present rather than the future. Other topical issues might be the use of ID cards, or punishing parents for the behaviour of their children or the issues surrounding the ban on hunting, for example.

The children should then formulate their ideas which they will translate into a front-page news article using Microsoft Office, Microsoft Word or Textease, for example, and show them how to create and write their articles in columns and blocks. Use the tool bar to insert pictures or sounds or tables which they could import from the Internet. The finished pieces of work may be printed out in hardcopy for display with the electronic copy saved for view if it incorporates sound and moving images.

CREATING A NEWSPAPER FRONT PAGE USING ICT

WORD-PROCESSING

The objective here is to help the children improve their keyboard skills, and the best way is to have them write a letter, since this will also be useful in having them learn the conventions of layout, salutation and conclusion. You could, for example, give them the task of writing a letter to their MP, or the headteacher or class teacher, to explain their feelings about:

- what they think of their school day
- would they like shorter hours?
- would they like an earlier start and an earlier finish?
- do they want more timetabling or less timetabling?
- would they want different teachers for different subjects?
- what about different kinds of lesson – what would they suggest?
- what do they think about school uniform?
- what about punishment for wrongdoers?

The specific skills you are aiming to have the children exercise will be in:

- using address blocks
- using correct salutations
- making amendments
- using spellings check
- creating paragraphs
- setting correct line spacing
- using the view layout
- signing off with signature block.

A very good exercise to help the children gain competence and confidence in using ICT will be for them to use Microsoft Draw, Textease, or similar art packages to create designs of their own which they can then print out. The objective is for them to think up a design for a wallpaper for their bedroom or a duvet cover or roller blind or curtain for their bedroom. They should be expected to create the design on screen using ICT. Some of the skills they could develop will be for them to make the design using the characteristics of the software, drawing, importing shapes, changing the design, rotating, erasing, filling in individual colours, inserting background colour, drawing in shapes of the articles such as the curtains or the duvet cover or the bedroom and then printing their work. Much of this kind of work can be really exciting, very attractive, absorbing and useful in helping children to develop confidence and competence in developing their artistic ideas.

ICT ART WORK

Music

HELP WITH MUSIC

Since I am musically dyslexic, I try my best to avoid teaching music, but there is always the time when there is no alternative but to face the music lesson. I did find that there is a lot of support and good ideas using the Internet, and the BBC site, www.bbc.co.uk/schools/4-11/music, was most interesting, fun and absorbing. Its appeal is that it is lively and interactive and encourages children to have fun while exploring basic musical concepts in sound, rhythm and mood. The site provides the teacher with lesson plans, learning outcomes, tips on classroom management, technical tips and cross-curricular links for your music sessions. You just need to make sure that, if you have to cover a music session, then you can have access to the ICT suite.

Should you find that you are not able to use the Internet, you could play a music CD or tape which the children might not know, such as for example, Clannad, or Enya or Fleetwood Mac, maybe even Khachaturyan or Stokowski, for example. Get the children to listen, to see if they can identify any musical instruments being used and ask them to write what the music evoked for them. Get them to think especially of moods, feelings, colours or 'pictures' in their mind. They should be encouraged to talk about their feelings and write what they found the music evoked for them.

Alternatively, I would suggest that you prepare for the music lesson by exploring good bookstores which have a section on primary education, for any hints on music or use the DfES and the BBC sites.

If, however, you are fortunate enough to be musical and you wish to use your talent and skills to enhance the music session for the children then I would advise you be creative. Do not feel bound to follow the set plan to the letter. As a teacher I applauded the supply teacher who used their initiative to bring a lesson to life.

Hints: It will pay you to get in to school early or to use your lunchtime to check what software the school has installed on its network and what use you could make of what is available. It is even possible that what you pick up in one school will be very useful in another which is in the same Local Education Authority.

Ask a member of staff for help – that is, if you do not have any guidance or materials left for you. Ensure that you are aware of which music sessions you must follow implicitly and which may be open to improvisation. If you are going to be creative then:

¶ ask or look for the musical instruments in the store/music resources cupboard
¶ plan your session using simple instruments
¶ carefully select your instrumentalists – you could check who has music lessons
¶ lead your session so that you direct; this will help you to keep control and ensure the enjoyment of your class.

It is worth remembering that many a successful session has come out of taking a simple song or nursery rhymes, sea shanties, action songs, which you can then have fractions of the class perform in 'rounds' or have basic rhythmic clapping or the occasional tambourine or bongo.

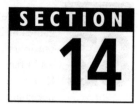

PE, games
and dance

INTRODUCING PE

It is entirely possible that you will be expected to take a games or PE lesson, either in the school hall or gym, or outdoors on the field or playground. Some schools try to avoid having the supply teacher take this sort of practical lesson for the simple reason that good control is necessary and if you do not know the children it may prove problematic.

Common practice in most schools, therefore, is to avoid putting the supply teacher in a situation where a good knowledge of the children is vital to their well-being. This generally means that you *may not* have to take games or PE but be prepared, just in case.

In actuality, however, a pragmatic approach rationalizes that as a qualified teacher you should be able to cope in all circumstances and conditions so that situations may occur when you find yourself with a period of games, dance, swimming or PE on your timetable.

You would be well advised to make sure that you are aware of any possible dangers or shortcomings in the space where you will expect the children to be mobile and active, so, if at all possible,

- look over the room, hall, gym or play area where the session is to take place
- check for possible hazards in the form of furniture and obstacles, and for clear, clean floor space
- create a good proportion of clear space for the safe conduct of your activities
- think about where you will seat those not taking part for whatever reason
- work out where you will position the miscreants for a temporary exclusion, time out or for 'reflective' purposes – so that they cannot influence/distract the other children.
- decide on how you will occupy those children not taking part for whatever reasons.

KNOW YOUR WORKSPACE

Plan your session with a warm-up exercise, then for the session:

¶ consider how you will select teams – all boys/girls or mixed teams – will you let the children select?

¶ plan how you will introduce the activity – explain the objectives/outcomes

¶ know in advance what rules *you* will apply and how to score

¶ more importantly, plan out how you will control the session – issues of sportsmanship, fair play, obeying the set rules and on penalties for any transgressions.

Find out what you will be able to do with the disruptive element or an accident – should this occur.

Always remember to begin these sessions with a warm-up exercise designed to stretch muscles, get the children breathing deeply, their muscles warmed, the children conditioned to the activities and to ensure that the children suffer no painful muscle/tendon sprains, which can occur when rapid or sustained movement is demanded of 'cold' muscles.

¶ have the children jog gently around the perimeter of the field/playground and follow this up with a faster lap

¶ play tag – start with one child as 'it' who is then joined by other children as they are 'tagged' and who now have to tag others until all the children have been caught/tagged

¶ select one child to be the 'hare' and set him/her running first then get the class to chase and catch the 'hare'

¶ if indoors, get them to lie on their tummies on the floor and attempt 5 press-ups or they could lie on their backs, raising their heels about 15cm off the floor – repeated 5 times, or they could do simple bending and stretching exercises, twisting on the spot – trunk rotations, reaching up, touching toes

¶ they should try 'travelling' about the floor space using different movements or keeping to mats laid on the floor.

These exercises can be used either for warm-up at the start of a session or for cooling down at the end of the session.

Rounders is a game played on the field in good weather, and which is familiar to all children and is played to very simple rules. Essentially the bowler throws the ball to the batter who hits it and runs in rotation to each of three equidistant bases in the field of play. Standing at each of the bases is a fielder whose task it is to prevent the batter alighting on his/her base by catching the ball and touching the batter before s/he actually stands on the base. The batter has to try to make an unbroken run through all three bases and back to the batting point to achieve a 'rounder'. The fielders should try to catch the ball and throw it to the base fielder. A point is scored for each 'rounder'. If in doubt, let the class organize the game and rules but you set the teams and adjudicate.

¶ Keep the rules simple – two equal mixed teams, each batter has three strikes with the bat. A full catch of a flighted ball or a 'tag' (touched with the ball in the hand of the field player on the base) and the batter is out.

¶ Keep all of the children involved and watch those waiting to bat. Keep the game moving, even if you have to remake the rules, so as to ensure that those waiting to bat do not have too long a wait. Children will get cold with no exercise especially sitting in PE kit, and boredom is always assured for those without a purpose.

¶ Keep strong control of those waiting to bat by deducting points or runs for excessive noise, chatting, inattention or behavioural infringements. I have found this to be a really effective strategy as it helps to keep the children focused on the game and also is a means to encourage good sportsmanship as they witness and applaud the achievement of the players. Without this control the children will sit and gossip or be inattentive, or simply misbehave or play.

¶ Be aware of where the fielders are and of what they are doing. Make sure no one is able to walk off the field or simply sit making daisy chains.

¶ Use any children who are not taking part because of no kit or who have a sick note as recorders taking down the scores.

Hint: You will need five cones, two bats and two balls. The children will know the rules but you have the final word on decisions. You score by making a full 'rounder'.

This is a game of netball without nets. A really great idea for supply teachers because you will only need a ball, two benches and 5 bibs or bands to identify the teams. The rules are simple; the ball has to be passed to a player in a position to score. While a player has the ball s/he is not permitted to move their feet. The bench (target) player must catch the ball tossed by his team mates and this will allow the player of the successful pass to stand with the bench player, on the bench to become a second target.

- ¶ Divide the class into teams of 5 players
- ¶ One player from one team of each pair of teams stands *on* a bench at the back of the court, in the *opponents'* half. What s/he has to do is to catch the ball, thrown by a team mate, over the heads of the defending team
- ¶ The court players now pass the ball to each other using simple netball rules on travelling
- ¶ A score is to pass the ball into the hands of the player on the bench who can move about the bench to catch any pass
- ¶ The player making a successful pass joins his team mate on the bench, so there are now two players on the bench
- ¶ Play proceeds until all of the winning team stand on the bench in the opponents' half

Hint: Split the class into teams of five and space the teams around the court to ensure that you have smaller groups where boisterous physical over-exuberance is less likely.

IDEA 87

BUCKETBALL

This game is something I have developed from observing other games and taking aspects from some and making my own rules as I went along, observing how the children could be fully, physically involved. The beauty of this game is that virtually all of the children will be fully physically and mentally involved.

The basic game plan is similar to rounders with the same field layout of three bases, the batter's position and the bowler's position.

The bowler, supported by two catchers, standing by the bucket, bowls underarm, three balls in quick succession at the batter. The batter has to hit every one of the balls and then run to first post. The fielders have to catch all of the balls and throw them to the catchers and bowler whose part now is to return the balls to the bucket to arrest the run of the batter. The bucket remains on the floor at all times.

Should all three of the balls not be placed in the bucket, the batter can keep running and a 'rounder' is scored. The batter will otherwise remain on the base which they reached when the balls were collected in the bucket.

No player is 'out' but the whole batting team is 'out' on one clean catch by an individual fielder and the fielding team will now bat.

This is a really quick team game with possible rapid 'turn around' which will ensure that all of the children can expect to be taking part in the activity at least once before the end of the session.

In this game, even those children lacking refined coordination, facing three balls bowled in quick succession and with the distractions of balls being chased by fielders and catchers, and by overthrows, will forget that they lack skill as they simply swing at three balls coming their way.

The desired outcome is for the balls to travel far when hit, so the children will have the exercise of running to field the balls, collecting, throwing and catching, as well as batting.

Hint: You will need one bucket, three balls, preferably tennis or *hard* sponge balls and five cones. The harder the balls the further they fly and the more the fielders have to work and the more exciting the game as you see balls and children fly all over the field.

I D E A

88

FOOTBALL

Football is always a good standby, providing vigorous exercise for all and the rules are indisputable and universally known and understood in the playground. You will also need the minimum of equipment with four balls and perhaps bibs or bands to identify the teams.

¶ Keep the teams small – around 6/8 on each side is advised so that no child has the opportunity to stand uninvolved.

¶ Keep the playing area restricted, so that you have good control and so that you don't have a runaway ball carrier who does not know how to change direction. Half a netball pitch is an ideal playing area for the small team games.

¶ Try to aim to have two games going as this will involve the whole class and you can also be sure that no child is going to be cold or bored.

¶ Try separating the class into boys' and girls' teams – if you have equal numbers – then mix the teams once the children have 'warmed-up'.

¶ Use any non-participating children as 'referees' since this will keep them occupied and there will also be the element of 'control' on each pitch.

¶ Make sure before you start that you make it plain to the children what your expectations are regarding behaviour, rules, noise, participation and sportsmanship.

¶ Keep strong control by maintaining a presence on the pitch(es) and making decisions regarding any disputes.

Hints: Define the playing area. Have each pair of teams playing in half a netball pitch. The idea here is to help the children develop their control skills by restricting the playing boundaries. Aim to have four teams, so it may be that you will have between 6 and 8 players in a team, which will be enough to absorb the whole of the class. You decide in which teams you will place any 'odd' players if numbers are not 'tidy'. You will have two 'games' to supervise and, setting the games in two halves of the netball pitch, you should move between both games imposing your presence, keeping the rules and the peace and making sure that no individual is avoiding the exercise.

This is a very interesting and fun way of exercising. Basically the idea is:

¶ Divide the class into 4 teams. You are aiming to have between 6 and 8 players in each team.

¶ Each player has a PE band tucked into the back of their shorts/tracksuit/jogger bottoms. The objective is for the opposing players to 'capture' this band from the ball player to claim the ball. This capture is the tackle.

¶ The teams use a rugby ball which they pass – underarm if you wish – to a team mate. Players must *not* pass the ball on a run. They should stop, look for a team mate, make the pass and *then* run into a position to receive a pass. There are no restrictions on the direction of the passes.

¶ The opposing team players have to *capture the PE band* from the *ball carrier* in order to effect change-over and claim the ball for their play. They can only claim the PE band while the player has the ball.

¶ The overall objective of the game is to *place* the ball down *behind* the opponents' base line for a try.

¶ The winning team is the one with the most tries in the time you have allotted.

Hint: Apply the strategies on team structure, definition of playing area and control which I have outlined for football to help you with touch rugby.

TOUCH RUGBY

INDOOR PUCK HOCKEY

A very good standby for those sessions when the inclement weather precludes games outdoors is to have a game of indoor hockey. You will need a puck or a flight ball, both of which are plastic and lightweight and should be standard equipment in the school, 10 plastic hockey sticks and two standard benches. Have all of your equipment ready at hand before the session. The benches are placed on their sides at either end of the hall and these are the 'goal' against which the puck or flight ball is to be struck to score a goal. Teams are to attack and to defend their 'goal'.

- Take your class into the hall and lead the warm-up exercises (see Idea 84).
- Divide your class into mixed teams of five labelled 1, 2, 3, 4, 5 (if you have a big class).
- Have teams sit along the sides of the hall with even number teams sitting opposite the odd number teams
- Place the flightball/puck in the centre of the hall with 5 sticks in either half of the court.
- Instruct the children that as you call out their team they are to run from their start position around behind the designated 'goal' (bench), pick up their sticks and attempt to score by hitting the puck/ball against their opponents' bench to score the goal. Direct each team to run in opposite directions around the perimeter.
- Call out two teams, say 1 and 3 or 3 and 4, or 2 and 5. The teams will run out and the 5-minute game begins. The goal is scored.
- Blow your whistle to end the game. Teams lay down their sticks neatly in their own half.
- Select the next two teams and follow the same routine.
- Record the winners and conclude with the play-off between the winning teams.

The central focus of this kind of exercise is to aim to help the children exercise their imaginations as they develop their physical coordination, learn to express themselves and develop self-confidence and enjoyment of physical exercise.

¶ Take in a CD or tape cassette of gentle mood music such as Enya, Clannad, popular classics or any non-vocal sound track.

¶ Get the children changed and then do some simple warm-up exercises such as stretching, turning, spinning, moving, travelling . . .

¶ Sit the children 'in a space' and play the music. Ask the children to think of pictures/animals, a game . . . whatever they can imagine/feel/see coming from the music. Ask them to visualize images from the sounds they are hearing.

¶ Play the music again and have the children act out what they felt, saw, thought when they listened to the music.

¶ Stop the music, and select individuals to articulate and demonstrate their routines.

¶ Have the children repeat the exercise, make additions and alterations or refinements, then demonstrate changes.

¶ Play a track from any of the music mentioned above. Get the children to listen to the music, then ask them to imagine the music describing the movement of an animal. Having planted the idea of an animal move-ment in their minds, play the music again and have the children imagine what it would be like to be:
¶ a cat creeping silently
¶ an elephant moving gracefully, purposefully, ponderously
¶ a mouse – furtive, frightened, bold, secretive
¶ an owl – hunting, gliding noiselessly, confidently
¶ or have them move like the animal which they imagined they 'saw' or imagined in the music

¶ Have the children work individually to create their own impressions of the imagined animal movement they 'saw' in the music. Select any who would like to act out their movement to the class.

- Build on this phase by having the children work in small groups of three to four to make up a dance drama sequence putting their 'creations' together in one whole. Encourage them to discuss and plan what they will do and who will do what.
- Use floor mats to make up a floor gymnastics exercise to the music. Each group is to be confined to their own mat.
- Use floor mats – without any music and have the children find different ways of moving over each mat using different parts of their bodies.
- Observe the groups closely then choose a group with interesting/imaginative ideas with a view to have it demonstrate their movement to the class.
- Signal the class to 'finish your exercise – then stop' and have all the groups sit quietly for the demonstration.

Hint: Aim to end the session in plenty of time to include the demonstrations and changing back into school uniform/clothes in comfortable time for the next session. Remember the essentials of the warm-up and warm-down exercises before and after the activity.

Behaviour management

IDEA

92

BE PROACTIVE

The best way to avoid any behaviour problems is to take ownership of the classroom and the lesson. Keep the children active, busy, interested and you will be able to obviate/forestall any problems in the classroom. Always look for opportunities to use positive motivation based on activities which the children find worthwhile so that as they succeed you are able to give rewards in the form of praise, positive comment, stickers, stamps or reports to the class teacher or headteacher. The following ideas may help to get the best out of the child without needing to resort to sanctions and negative reinforcement:

- ¶ Ensure the children are purposefully engaged in work.
- ¶ Ensure that every child has sufficient work to keep them occupied and learning.
- ¶ Make clear that you will expect high standards of work from every child and that you intend to leave examples of the work for the class teacher to examine.
- ¶ Do not accept sub-standard work. Read over and correct the work, then insist that the child rewrite the work out in best, correcting the mistakes you had outlined. Let the children know when their work does not meet your standards and expectations.
- ¶ Award points, stickers or fun stamps for good work and good behaviour.
- ¶ Mark work as it is being undertaken and make written comments.

Should you find that you have behaviour problems, aim to modify behaviour by dealing with the individual yourself in the first instance:

¶ In the event that a child produces obviously unacceptable work, ask him/her to give the work marks out of 10. If the marks given are low, ask what s/he thinks needs to be done to raise the marks and ask them to make the revision. If the child chooses to express complete satisfaction, ask what mark or comment the class teacher would give the work, then ask what the class teacher would expect for the work to achieve a higher mark.

¶ Should you consider the behaviour of a child to be marginally unacceptable then a stern warning to show what is unacceptable and what you expect instead.

¶ For behaviour which you consider, for example, to be obviously against school and/or your standards, you should award a detention of no more than 10 minutes.

¶ For those individuals who very obviously are wasting time award a detention of between 3 and 5 minutes for them to finish the set task, then set them to copying out 5 words relating to behaviour from a dictionary and writing five sentences using these words.

CHANGING THEIR BEHAVIOUR

SCHOOL SUPPORT

In the event that you know that none of the sanctions mentioned in the previous idea will work to secure the desired behaviour or to stop/ease the disruption to the class, you must as soon as possible send for or send the child to a senior member of the permanent staff. The important issue here is to involve a senior member of staff, since this will ensure that it is clear to the class that you do have support and that you are prepared to use this support. Just as important is making the staff aware of the kind of disruption/unacceptable behaviour any individual or group of individuals may be causing.

An experience I had while working on supply in a school in south London necessitated my having to report the behaviour of a child to the office of the headteacher. As a result, I received a letter of apology from the school and one from the pupil concerned. It was noted that the child had a record of misbehaviour and had been warned about his behaviour toward supply teachers and the school had now instituted a form of report procedure which would ensure that no other supply teachers would be subject to his provocative behaviour.

- Remember that you are a teacher and therefore a member of staff, and you will not tolerate bad behaviour of any sort. Don't turn a 'blind eye'. Be firm, fair and consistent from the outset so that you establish your authority which will be backed by the authority of the school.

- Always make sure that the sanctions you impose are practicable, and if you make a threat of imposition of a sanction you actually apply that sanction or you will lose credibility. It is absolutely essential that if you issue a threat or a promise of sanction that you actually carry out that threat or sanction.

- Always ensure that you do not back a child into a corner – figuratively speaking. Give the child room for doubt, time to think. Instead of saying 'I am ordering you to sit down now!' say something like
  - 'if you are not going to sit down now I shall ignore you'
  - 'if you are not going to sit down now I will have your chair removed'
  - 'if you are not going to sit down now I will not allow you to take part in the lesson'
  - 'if you are not going to sit down now you will leave the classroom and sit with the headteacher'

Find out what school strategies and policies exist regarding minor discipline infringements as in, for example, poor work, inattentiveness, disobedience or simple disrespect for you as a teacher. The way in which you respond to any given situation will condition the way the children behave and what they will learn about how they might exploit or conform to what they perceive to be strength or weakness.

Be prepared to use the school as a resource to ensure that you don't have to begin basic classroom discipline from scratch. The strategy which I found to be most effective was to let the children know that I was a qualified teacher, and that I was in their classroom to teach them. I emphasized the point that I was not there to provide a class-minding service, so my expectations were that they should work as normal and that I was not paid to amuse or simply keep them occupied. I made it plain that I would not tolerate any behaviour which would be unacceptable to their teacher and any such uncharacteristic behaviour would be reported, firstly to the headteacher and then in a written report left for their class teacher to deal with on her/his return. You should find that in using this particular strategy you will be setting the parameters, expectations and behavioural standards from the outset because the children will know that what is expected of them will be exactly what is expected of them on a daily basis – something with which they are familiar.

Setting and demanding high standards of work and behaviour will enable you to teach effectively, make the learning experiences of the children enjoyable and worthwhile and will help you to build up your own professional reputation, standing and demand in schools.

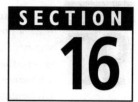

Making the most of your day

PROFESSIONALISM

As a matter of professional courtesy you should always leave a note for the class teacher outlining what work you have done, how far you got, what sort of follow-up is possible and, if necessary, the names of the children who are worthy of note, either for reward or for cautioning. As a class teacher I found this sort of feedback invaluable because I was able to work from what the children had covered with their supply teacher. I often used the information provided in the notes to reinforce what was covered, building up on or leading on from the ideas which sometimes served as my introduction to follow-up work.

Make sure you mark all the work the children have done for you. Write positive comments so that you are giving encouragement, feedback and motivation. Children really look forward to the comments made in their books because they know that the teacher has taken time to read the work and therefore the efforts they made were worthwhile. Comments also help the child to learn from the mistakes you have marked, from the corrections you outline and from any positive comments made regarding what it is they have done well. For your own benefit, should you return to the school, the children will remember not only the written comments you made but also that the work they completed for you was appreciated. In addition to the written comments you should make it your personal practice to award stickers or use stamps as reward or encouragement to emphasize and highlight your comments.

MARKING AND MOTIVATING

Make sure you tidy the classroom so that it is left as tidy as you would expect to find it yourself. It was a real frustration, on returning to school, to find that I was having to spend extra time and effort to tidy my classroom which had been treated in a very cavalier fashion by the supply teacher who had not been professionally courteous enough to leave the classroom as I had left it for their use. Discussion of the merits of the supply teacher in staff meetings usually were instrumental in decisions as to whether they were 'listed' and invited to return or not.

Remember that the school will be judging you throughout the day. Key issues will be:

- how you present yourself
- how you control the class
- whether the children are on task
- the work the children produce at the end of the day
- your drive, motivation and involvement

Enjoy the day. I'm sure you will not need reminding that at the end of the day you go home – there will be no meetings, no extra-curricular commitments, no school plays or discos and, more importantly, no planning – short-term, medium-term or long-term and, of course, no accountability to the governors, only to yourself as a professional and to the agency from whom you secure your employment.

CREATING AN IMPRESSION